T0171677

Also by Jason Johnson:

I Hate Bush and So Do You (2003)

You Make a Good Point...Bonehead! (2007)

Other stuff that no one has read (1970-present)

HERE'S ANOTHER DAMN BOOK THAT NO ONE WILL READ

The Unexpurgated Zenith City
Essays, 2007-2010

Jason Johnson

authorHOUSE®

AuthorHouse™
1663 Liberty Drive
Bloomington, IN 47403
www.authorhouse.com
Phone: 1-800-839-8640

© *2011 Jason Johnson. All rights reserved. Some lefts, too.*

ISBN: 978-1-4567-2910-3 (sc)
ISBN: 978-1-4567-2909-7 (e)

No part of this book may be reproduced, stored in a retrieval system, or transmitted by any means, electronic, mechanical, photocopying, recording, fingerpainting, crayon, passed on by oral tradition, or anything else for that matter, without written consent from the author, who will most likely grant it because he has nothing better to do. Why not just ask? Also, this book is not a part of this complete breakfast, nor is it among the four major food groups, or any part of that new-fangled "food pyramid," whatever the hell that's supposed to be.

First published by AuthorHouse 02/03/2011

Library of Congress Control Number: 2011901795
Printed in the United States of America

Any people depicted in stock imagery provided by Thinkstock are models, and such images are being used for illustrative purposes only. Certain stock imagery © Thinkstock.

This book is printed on acid-free paper.

Because of the dynamic nature of the Internet, any Web addresses or links contained in this book may have changed since publication and may no longer be valid. The views expressed in this work are solely those of the author and do not necessarily reflect the views of the publisher, and the publisher hereby disclaims any responsibility for them.

ACKNOWLEDGMENTS AND DEDICATION:

AS SOON AS I THINK I'm out they pull me back in. That's what I thought when I was approached by Jennifer Martin-Romme in 2007 about writing for a new alternative newspaper, the *Zenith City Weekly* [sic]. (The paper, in fact, comes out every three weeks; but I suppose *Zenith City Every Three Weeks* doesn't quite have the same ring to it.) As you know, Jen, I believe that writers and editors were never meant to like each other—it violates Nature's order. Your patience, support, and sense of humor have made you frustratingly easy to work with, and that just makes me despise you all the more. I'm sure you understand. In fact, you *would* understand, because that's just *so* like you.

Although I was not eager to jump back into the alternative newspaper world, I was induced to come to the *Zenith* after being told that I would again be working with Richard Thomas, who enlisted me back in 2000 to write for his then-employer, the *Reader Weekly*. Richard: I'm sure you realize that, despite my gratitude for your encouragement and tutelage, our relationship will one day come to blows. You know it, and I know it. Until that day, my good friend, rue the day you met me. Rue it, I say!

Also, a tip of the hat to our sales staff. I know I haven't made your job of obtaining advertisers any easier with my columns about Jesus, farts, or Jesus's farts. My sincere thanks for enduring the constant slamming of doors in your face.

This book is lovingly dedicated to Sarah Palin. Hot, sexy, plain-spoken, and utterly batshit crazy. What would a political humorist do without you? Also, thanks for reading our newspaper, which I know you do, because you told Katie Couric that you read *all of them*. Now please run for president. Thank you.

TABLE OF CONTENTS

HERE'S ANOTHER DAMN INTRODUCTION THAT EVERYONE WILL SKIP OVER

IT IS OBVIOUS THAT I am a failed writer. I don't say that to be self-pitying; after all, Goebbels was a failed writer, and look how well he turned out! Everyone remembers him!

But in case I sound self-deprecating or engaging in false modesty—a trait, you will learn, that is not remotely in my character—I direct attention to my sales figures: My last three book projects sold fewer than two dozen copies each.

Now, I know what you're saying, or what you would be saying if anyone were reading this: An author could sell more than two dozen copies to family and friends alone. That would be correct, if I had that many friends. Besides, most of the friends-and-family demographic get free copies from me when a new book emerges, which is just as well, because otherwise they'd never buy one.

I did have one friend "buy" three copies of one of my books…but never paid me. My girlfriend doesn't read my work (see chapter 10), because she doesn't think I'm funny. My previous book, *You Make a Good Point…Bonehead!*, has sat on my parents' bookshelf for the past four years with a bookmark permanently resting in chapter 5.

In other words, unlike other self-published authors, I do not have a built-in audience. When I say, "Here's another damn book that no one will read," I'm not talking out of my ass.

So one may ask: Why, then, do I continue to publish books that basically amount to really expensive public journals? To which I answer: One should mind one's own business and shut one's damn piehole.

Ironically, my first book was my best-seller, even though it was by far the worst thing I've published. Fortunately, it sold a mere 600 copies—which, while a runaway smash compared to my other books, is still a disastrously low number. It did, however, give me my one lame celebrity story.

The book was a fluff piece on a famous pop star. (In fairness to myself, all books about this particular celebrity were fluff pieces during this largely pre-Internet era. A scholarly, journalistic biography would not be written until, I believe, about 2007.) The celebrity in question did not contact me himself, but I did come to the attention of his high-profile attorney, Lee Eastman.

For Beatle historians, it was Eastman whom Paul McCartney wanted as The Beatles' manager; the other Beatles wanted Allen Klein. In other words, it was Eastman, not Yoko Ono, who truly broke up The Beatles.

This is not to say Yoko isn't a horrible bitch. She absolutely is. But it goes without saying that a man who broke up the world's greatest musical act would have no trouble breaking the spine of an unknown writer who was, at that time, quite literally living in his parents' basement.

I had contacted the artist's record company regarding the copyright issues involved in reprinting a press release.

Now, you may be saying, "But there *are* no copyrights on press releases; they're written for maximum public disclosure. Copyrighting them would be counter-intuitive." At least, I'm guessing you're saying that, because you're most likely smarter than my then-publisher, which was run by, to put it charitably, slime-sucking morons.

My publisher wanted proof that the press release was public domain, which is what I requested from Mr. Eastman. Said Eastman, "We want to read the manuscript first."

This struck me as odd. After all, he was an attorney. Why did he have to read the entire manuscript to be sure that a press release was in the public domain? But I said yes, probably because I was simply flattered that someone, even an attorney, wanted to read my work.

So I sent him the manuscript. And waited. And waited.

Six months later, I got my answer from Eastman: "We're not going to endorse this book."

That, of course, was not the issue. "What about the press release?" I asked.

"Yeah, that's public record."

Which, I remind you, is something he could have told me six months earlier.

Asshole.

Yeah, that's right: I called a powerful celebrity attorney an asshole. What's he going to do? Read this book? I don't bloody think so.

So a failed writer I may be. But you know what? Beats being a dick of a lawyer who broke up The Beatles.

I'm done.

Jason Johnson
Fall 2010

I'LL SEE YOU ALL IN HELL!

GENERALLY AVOID WRITING ABOUT MY personal life, and not just because of privacy issues, although I have no intention of telling the world just how many hours of my day are consumed watching *Spongebob Squarepants*. No, I'm a private person because, in the words of Lincoln, "No one gives a crap." Besides, my life is a lot like a Republican presidential debate: There's almost no action, and if anyone started to pay close attention, they'd probably throw up.

But I will reveal this much: I'm 36 and I've been seeing a woman who's 21. Why is this important? Because I'm 36 and she's 21. How often does a guy like me get to hook up with a woman that young and not wind up on *Dateline*'s "To Catch a Predator"?

It's not just the age difference: I'm atheist and she's Roman Catholic, which results in some interesting theological discussions, to be sure. I once asked her if she felt that my heretical beliefs were my ticket to Hell. "No," she said, "because you're a good person, and I'll be praying for you, so you'll get into Heaven anyway."

"So I get a free pass in this life?" I asked.

"No, you don't get a 'free pass.' You still have to be a good person—" She stopped, perhaps realizing to whom

1

she was talking. "OK, you might go to Purgatory, but you'll be fine."

Ah, Purgatory! That puts me in the same unpainted, spartanly furnished room with unwed mothers, unbaptized children, and, I think, Rudy Giuliani.

Actually, that's not quite true: The Catholic Church only recently changed its position on unbaptized children, saying that they're now allowed into Heaven instead of going to Purgatory. I could point out that this is proof positive that organized religion is just making crap up as it goes along. After all, either babies have been sitting it out in Purgatory for thousands of years, or they haven't. And if they haven't, why did we think they were? Could it possibly be that the Church was talking out of their holy receptacles?

I could say that, but I won't. Because let's face it: Unbaptized babies are the scum of the earth.

Worse, the Catholic Church sure is turning into a bunch of bleeding-heart sissies. First, we allow unbaptized children into Heaven; next it'll be pro-abortionist, femi-nazi hippies, or as they're more commonly called, Hillary Clinton.

It is, in fact, a sign that the church has had to bend to 21st-century realities. In 2004, my girlfriend supported John Kerry, another Catholic who was pro-choice, pro-birth control, and pro-gay rights. I believe there's a word for Catholics like that. They're called Protestants.

The election of Pope Benedict hasn't made Catholicism any easier to swallow, certainly not among Islamic nations. Benedict began his term by quoting the Byzantine emperor Paleologos, who called Islam "evil and inhuman." Now, keep in mind that I haven't read Benedict's actual speech in his dead native tongue; I'm like Dan Quayle when he visited Latin America: "I sure wish I learned to speak Latin!"

(In case you're under 25, yes, Dan Quayle really said that. Thank your God that he didn't become president. Put a dumb guy in charge and who knows *what* might happen!)

Anyway, the Paleologos comment was apparently not condemned by the Pope, only referenced before springboarding onto a larger topic. This leads me to believe he was a great conversation stopper at parties:

Benedict: Yes, this reminds of something Hermann Goering used to say. He used to say, "Jews should suck it and die!"

Host [after long awkward pause]: Um, what does this have to do with *American Idol*?

Benedict: Oh, nothing, nothing. I just thought I'd quote Hermann Goering for no reason whatsoever. By the way, you wanna know what Michael Richards said about black people?

Host: Can I see your invitation?

The Pope also recently reminded his followers that Hell still exists, although today it's more commonly known as the DMV.

But back to my girlfriend and her Catholicism. She asked me why I was worried about going to Hell. I said, "I'm not worried. I'm just curious about you believe."

She told me, "I believe what my priest believes."

"Oh," I said, "so you believe that altar boys are sexy?"

OK, I didn't really say that. Even if Hell doesn't exist, she would've made one for me right then and there. Besides, that's totally unfair: There are thousands of Catholic priests out there, and only half of them molest children.

And I suspect that, despite her assertion to the contrary, I'm probably going to Hell. But like Billy Joel says, "I'd rather laugh with the sinners than cry with the saints." Besides, it's got to be better than Purgatory, with no one around to change all those unbaptized diapers except Rudy Giuliani.

I'm done.

VOTE BERGSON!
IT'LL BE FUNNY!

[*During his one and only term as mayor of Duluth, MN, Herb Bergson received a DUI after ramming his car into a bridge abutment. Bergson had previously been a police officer and mayor of Superior, WI.*]

A S A LIBERAL, I HAVE to say that Bush is the worst self-inflicted wound this country has ever suffered, setting back social and economic justice, foreign policy, and environmental standards in ways I never dreamed.

But as a comedian, I think he's pure gold.

In fact, part of me wishes he'd go ahead and declare martial law and rule in perpetuity, so I wouldn't have to dump the 90% of my repertoire that will have to go out the window if he ever left office. I could perform those jokes easily for the next thirty years or so, even if it would be only in front of a small crowd of my fellow Gitmo prisoners.

I'm not nearly as conflicted when it comes to Duluth mayor Herb Bergson, who is the only candidate I would ever vote for simply because I'm a comedian and I need the material. He's a bungler, but a likeable bungler, one who is, to quote Douglas Adams, mostly harmless. Incidentally,

Bergson can go ahead and use that slogan if he wishes: "Vote Bergson: He's innocuous!" Or, as David Letterman once suggested for Ross Perot: "C'mon! It'll be funny!"

This may seem as quite a switch from four years ago, when I called Bergson "an overexposed idiot" and "someone who sits on the fence so much his buttcheeks got splinters." [See my previous book, *You Make a Good Point...Bonehead!*] Actually, all those things said about Herb are still true. But I've looked over the top-tier mayoral candidates looking to replace him, and all are unfit to bring the hilarious escapades to the city that we've come to expect from our elected executives. Take a look at this graph showing previous Duluth mayors and their effect on local comedy material:

Mayor	Striking feature(s)	Comedic result
Ben Boo	Funny name	Chuckle (mostly during Halloween)
John Fedo	Crooked	Hilarious Nixon comparisons, tempered with disgust
Gary Doty	Bully, thug, power-mad	Pants-wetting convulsive laughter, tempered with bruises & scarring
Herb Bergson	Indecisive, inscrutable, more than slightly drunk	Side-splitting, asphyxiating laughter, causing milk to shoot out nose and undies to soil

As this graph clearly proves, Duluth has been greatly improving its laughter-to-misery ratio. Nothing encapsulates this more than Herb's driving "incident": Herb was apparently so drunk that I'm a little surprised his mugshot didn't show the lampshade over his head. And yet his accident caused only minor property damage, so we get all of this hilarity guilt-free! It's as if George W. Bush had all the policies of Bill Clinton, but still spoke like a dyslexic rhesus monkey. It's a liberal humorist's dream.

Remember the tomfoolery that was the Ten Commandments debate? Herb said he opposed removing the monument but would acquiesce to the decision of the city council, who he knew would be forced to remove it. That little joke became Herb's political equivalent of the "Who's-On-First" gag, upon which he would repeat endlessly. Like how he could give a gay rights speech while covering up gay art at the Depot; or how he could call for an audit of the Bayfront Blues Festival just before emails from Herb to the festival organizer surfaced with the header "wanna suck up?"—a prelude to Herb's illegal solicitation for free tickets. And we can't even prosecute him for that because, well, it's just ol' Herb! The only result to his screw-ups is a shrug of the shoulders followed by a comical "boing" sound.

I've looked over Herb's would-be replacements, and frankly, it's just sad. Oh, sure, supporters of city councilman and boyish classmate Don "Donny" Ness will point to his obvious political opportunism, culminating in the Machiavellian process in which he got his preferred candidate, Roger Reinert, elected to fill Bergson's vacant city council seat. But he's not "Donny" anymore, and he's not the kid-faced pecker that he used to be, which means there isn't that added element of comedy, as with the Stewie character from *Family Guy,* who at least is still cute when he tries to conquer the world.

Speaking of cartoon characters, there's Greg Gilbert, the Charlie Brown of the group, who always seems to have the mayor's office pulled away from him like a football–which, coincidentally, is also the same shape as Gilbert's head. Unfortunately, Gilbert's more sad than funny, as evidenced by the groan-inducing way fellow councilman Laurie Johnson puts him in a headlock until he coughs up his lunch money. He is not, shall we say, an alpha male. Neither is Meg Bye, whom most agree is a solid, competent, capable thinker—all of which means she's totally wrong for the job of Duluth's mayor.

Does all this mean I'll be voting for Herb? Of course not; I live outside Duluth, which only makes it all the better for me as an observer. After all, Laurel and Hardy are only funny if they're tearing up someone else's house.

I'm done.

ANOTHER VICTORY IN THE
WAR ON THE ENVIRONMENT

RENA SENDLER OF POLAND RESCUED over 2500 Jewish children from the Nazi occupation in WWII, not even surrendering the children's whereabouts after having her legs crushed in a vice and her bones shattered with hammers. Recently nominated for a Nobel Peace Prize, Sendler was passed over in favor of Al Gore. So congratulations to Gore, and to Ms. Sendler, I'd just like to say: Suck it, bitch!

No, no, I'm kidding of course. There's always next year! Wait, what's that? You're 97? Man, I guess that's another crushing defeat for you, then!

But yes, Al Gore is the 2007 NPP winner, earning himself a cash prize and a gold medal, both of which were quickly snatched away by Kathleen Harris. It is the topper in a good year for Gore, having recently won an Oscar for his documentary *An Inconvenient Truth*, plus a Guinness World Record for largest armpit sweat stains, besting the previous record holder, Richard Nixon, who in turn had bested another prominent American, Betty Davis.

It's fitting that Gore should receive the Nobel Peace Prize, because, after all, we're at war with the environment. Currently we're winning, but only because of weak congressional oversight of the administration's wiretapping procedures. Plus, we're aided by the American consumer, who took to heart President Bush's suggestion to do everything as normal, such as buying increasingly disposable consumer goods, and driving state to state in search of a place to dump the trash. Any deviation from the norm—other than providing limitless executive power, of course—and the environment wins.

In the "better late than never" category, it was heartening to see a recent CNN report describing global warming deniers as "few and far between," with anchorman Miles O'Brien even going as far as to say that most of these deniers were in the pockets of the fossil fuel industry. Yes, the Most Trusted Name in News has finally denounced global warming deniers, proving that the mainstream media has no trouble stating the cold, hard truth, as long as it is a truth that had been painfully stapled to most of their viewers' faces about the last twenty years, prompting many said viewers to turn to each other and say, "Ohhhhh, so that's what this 'WE'RE ALL GOING TO DIE' memo means!"

(Similarly, the media now feel free to ask questions about the sanity of Mr. Bush's War, questions like, "Why the hell didn't we ask questions four years ago?" Most readers will recall that media coverage of the conflict in 2003 was done with a fair balance that ranged from "sycophantic lapdog approval" to "boldface doggie-style leg humping." But now that's changed, because reporters have found their spine, which was buried below several tons of opinion polls showing the Denier-in-Chief with an approval rating of dirt%. But I digress.)

It's certainly good news that global warming is no longer in dispute by reasonable, educated thinkers. But thinkers seldom get talk shows, and that's where Glenn

Beck steps in. Beck likes to point to a petition of 17,000 scientists who claim that global warming is not real, a fact that sounds stunning until one realizes that the "scientists" include 16,991 refrigerator repairmen and nine unemployed stoners watching the Sci-Fi Channel.

Actually, that's unfair. The truth is much worse.

The petition was started ten years ago by an organization called the Oregon Institute of Science and Medicine, an impressive army of academians (and by "army," I mean, if you want to get technical, "six") who are all self-described "Christian Scientists," which the rest of the world generally refers to as "Not Scientists."

As for the rest of the signers, it breaks down like this: Some recanted; some claim they never signed it in the first place; and others are—again, we need to get technical—full of crap. In fact, a survey of the names by the magazine *Scientific American* found that, out of a hundred selected names, fewer than half did not have degrees in climatology or had no science degree at all, a piteous state equaled only by those who receive their degrees from the U of Minnesota-Duluth.

Of course, the OISM declared that all signers had degrees and that thorough background checks were performed, a claim that is in no way diminished by the signature of…Dr. B.J. Honeycutt. Yes, that's right: The fictional doctor from *M.A.S.H.* does not have a problem with global warming. Compelling, sure; but we all know that we should never take any petition seriously until it's authenticated directly from the mouth of Doogie Howser.

Fortunately, we don't rely on the OISM to institute environmental policy. That purview belongs to the Environmental Protection Agency. And I have no problem putting my faith in them, even if they recently lost a Supreme

Court case that said they had to—wait for it—protect the environment.

I'm not sure what surprises me more: that the EPA actually went to court to prevent themselves from doing their job; or the fact that it was a split decision, 5 to 4. Apparently, four justices found "Environmental Protection Agency" a little vague. If the justices can't even agree on what "protect" means, it must make ordering a pizza a real bitch: "Justices Souter, Bryer, and Ginsburg will have sausage and pepperoni. And Scalia, Thomas, and Roberts will have no workforce protections for homosexuals. With extra cheese."

But it's clear that the ice is thawing when discussing the subject of global warming with conservatives. The tide is turning, though sadly, it's turning into a tidal wave that can put Florida under a few fathoms—in which case, Gore can add one more trophy to his collection.

I'm done.

A CLINICAL CROSS-EVALUATION OF MAN'S BIOLOGICAL PROCESSES AND DIACHRONIC EVOLUTION... PLUS A LOT OF FART JOKES

ALTHOUGH THE HUMAN APPENDIX WAS long thought to be as useless as Democratic subpoena power, doctors now believe that it still serves some biological function, specifically, to become infected and gross the hell out of us. It can also be attached to the end of some fancy-schmancy book, although I find a freshly excised one can leave the pages all sticky.

It had previously been believed that the appendix was an evolutionary relic, an object we needed in times past, but now merely find disgusting, like John McCain. But doctors now say that this organ does, in fact, serve an evolutionary purpose. And if one wonders why we evolved something whose sole purpose is to become infected, when it would appear to run contradictory to the survival instinct, then one does not work for a pharmaceutical company.

And this leads me, in a way that only mothers of adolescent boys could understand, to the subject of farting.

13

I got to thinking (because I am clearly a thinking humorist) about why humans evolved the practice of farting. That is to say, I understand *why* we fart: Our food contains complex sugars called oligosaccharides, which are dissolved by the bacterial microfauna in our digestive tract, producing a methane build-up that is released through the rectal integument—

What? Yes, I am a fart expert. You people may have dates and spouses; I have fart books.

It was concluded, in a study that I have no wish to observe firsthand, that the average person farts ten to fifteen times a day. I do not wish to meet this person; and presumably, I never will, because he is most likely German. However, it is now proven once and for all that, despite your previous assessments of your co-workers, those people are exceptionally above average.

But again, why do we fart? After all, all human characteristics seem to have evolved for one of three purposes: to catch prey, to escape predators, and to mate. Farting does not seem to help any of these. And yet, somewhere along the evolutionary line, a male of the species—and I think we can all agree it was a male—said to himself, "Hmm, I notice that a half-hour after I eat, I begin to emit a noxious odor, one that alerts predators and prey to my presence and makes the females less willing to mate with me.

"On the other hand…I can light them on fire!" And that's how our common ancestor survived to pass down (so to speak) the farting gene: because he was really good at punctuating his campfire stories.

It's been argued that humans need to fart to survive, because otherwise gas would build up in the colon and rupturing an intestine, in what would have to be the most grizzly way to die from an overdose of brussel sprouts. But clearly, humans have no health reasons to fart; otherwise, women would fart. And we all know women don't fart.

Well, allow me to clarify: *attractive* women don't fart. I don't care what lies you want to spread about Jennifer Love Hewitt, but I can assure you that she's never passed a ghost whisper in her life. If, however, you had ever been locked in a closet with my grandmother, you'd have been having flashbacks to Auschwitz, even if you'd never set foot in Germany.

At this point, some men are probably looking at their girlfriends and thinking, "Am I dating a farter?" Perhaps you can better guess after looking at this chart:

NOT A FARTER	FARTER
Ashley Judd	Winona Judd
Ashley Olsen	Mary-Kate Olsen
Teri Hatcher, Eva Longoria	Marcia Cross, Felicity Huffman*
Kate Beckinsale in *Underworld*	Kate Beckinsale in *Pearl Harbor*
Kim Alexis, Sports Illustrated swimsuit model	Kim Alexis, mother and hemorrhoid sufferer

(*I'm not sure about Nicolette Sheridan. She may or may not be a farter; but if not, I give her no more than two years before she springs a leak in a Taco Bell ladies' room. There are other uncertain farters; for example, you can always tell when Scarlett Johansson has the farts, because she starts doing something really ugly with her hair.)

Also worth noting are the Bush Twins: Barb is not a farter. Jenna is a farter *and* a belcher. And Barbara Bush, the grandmother? Mega-farter, mega-belcher, and a walking, talking yeast infection.

I'm done.

YOUR SPOUSE, ROOMMATE, CO-WORKER: VICTIMS... OR SUPERVILLAINS?!

WHEN THE CHARACTER OF SPIDER-MAN was adapted for the big screen, he lost his webshooters, instead shooting webs directly from his arms. Well, that makes sense; after all, isn't that how spiders do it? Actually, I always thought they pooped their webs out, but I suppose that wouldn't give the filmmakers a PG-13 rating.

It would also make the action scenes unpleasantly short:

Spider-Man: Surrender, Doctor Octopus!

Doc Ock: I will never surrender to you, Spider-Man!

Spider-Man: Oh, I think you will. [Pulls down pants, points ass in Ock's direction.] This is what I call, "The Double Barrel!"

Doc Ock: All right! I surrender! Christ, why couldn't my arch-enemy be Ant-Man?!

I love the Spider-Man comics and films, but they are a textbook case of what we writers call the "conservation of characters." No character can be introduced unless they are either a supervillain or a future victim of a supervillain, which makes superhero family reunions very complicated and highly insured affairs. It also virtually guarantees that police will summoned even earlier than is usual at these functions, perhaps as soon as when the first hibachi is hurled over the Empire State Building.

The last Spider-Man film is a good example of this character conservation. Consider: Peter Parker's professional rival (Eddie Brock) just happens to be dating Peter's lab partner (Gwen Stacy) who is the daughter of the police captain (um, Captain Stacy, I presume), who just happens to be investigating the murder of Peter's Uncle Ben, who was shot by Flint Marko, who later becomes the Sandman, who apparently buys his clothes at the Turns-To-Sand Clothes Shop, which is owned by O.J. Simpson, who leaves to use the restroom just in time to be hit on by Larry Craig.

If such coincidences appear impossible, take this little quiz:

Which character, at some point in the Spider-Man comics, was NOT revealed to be The Green Goblin?

(A) Peter Parker's roommate
(B) Peter Parker's roommate's dad
(C) Peter Parker's roommate's psychiatrist
(D) the nephew of Peter Parker's co-worker
(E) Dick Cheney

The answer, of course, is (E). Dick Cheney was never The Green Goblin. He was, in fact, revealed to be Darth Maul from the Star Wars prequels.

It's also worth noting that Peter's ex-girlfriend, Betty Brant, married Ned Leeds, who was briefly The Hobgoblin, although it was later revealed after Leeds died that he had been framed by Roderick Kingsley, who had previously been an employer of Mary-Jane Watson, Peter's future wife and the niece of Anna Watson, who was neighbors with Aunt May, who just happened to have buried treasure in the basement of her house, which was sought after by a burglar, the same burglar who Peter could've stopped earlier that night, but couldn't, because he was too busy trying to read the cheat sheet to determine if the burglar was a supervillain or his long-lost step-cousin.

If you can't follow all of that, congratulations: You have a chance at reproducing.

As for the rest of you, yes, you read that right: Betty Brant is single again. Also that part about Aunt May having buried treasure in her basement, although that isn't the weirdest thing to happen in the series. See if you can guess which one of these things did NOT happen in the Spider-Man comics:

(A) Aunt May married Doctor Octopus

(B) Spider-Man died, only to be revealed later that he was merely molting

(C) Ronald and Nancy Reagan became scaly serpent people

(D) Dick Cheney killed Lex Luthor by shooting him in the face

Ha, ha! Actually, none of these things happened. Well, except (B). (B) definitely happened. But as for the rest: (A) is clearly ridiculous. *Of course* Aunt May didn't marry Doc Ock. They were merely engaged—Spider-Man broke up the wedding. (C) is also downright silly, and I assure you it did not happen in the *Spider-Man* series. It happened in *Captain America*. (Yep. Look it up.) And and as for (D), I'm clearly clowning around there. Lex Luthor is a DC character, not

Marvel. Besides, in this case, Cheney killed Luthor using a necktie and a broken crutch.

Granted, I'm engaging in a bit of snarky overanalysis. Comicbooks are meant to be read as pure fantasy, and suspension of disbelief is a requirement, much like Iraqi progress reports from the Bush administration. Besides, if a planted neo-con journalist in the White House press room turns out to moonlight as a gay website porn star, my surprise at bizarre secret identities is somewhat muted. So much so, in fact, that I didn't bat a lash at the identity of the new Joker.

No, no, it's not Dick Cheney! That's just silly. It's Laura.

I'm done.

ESCAPE FROM THE KIDDIE TABLE

ROWING UP ATHEIST, THERE WERE several ways to make the holiday season more enjoyable. The most obvious is to belt the Christian kids with snowballs and learn how much that "turn the other cheek" crap really stuck. (Answer: none.)

As an adult, I tolerate Xmas because it is close to Stan Lee's birthday on the 28th, a time-honored holiday in my household. It is a holiday that requires no church service or gift-giving, which, surprisingly enough, does not sit well with my orthodox Catholic girlfriend, especially the part about the gifts.

I never ask for gifts on the holidays for that reason, but I am calling in all those unpurchased presents and making one simple wish: I'm 36 years old, and I think I deserve to be moved from the Kiddie Table.

You folks know what I mean. At least, you do if you have a family, which is presumably everyone, unless you're Mitch McConnell and came from a spore. The dreaded Kiddie Table is that table at every holiday feast where the children are seated at their own table in the TV room, under the guise that they can watch cartoons together without getting into trouble, but is really for the purpose of reducing

Uncle Dave's need to drink. It always fails miserably on both levels.

I've spent many an Xmas dinner at the Kiddie Table, and I think I've earned the right to sit at the Grown-Ups Table. One gets tired of all the drooling, babbling, nose-running, and pants-wetting, to say nothing of the endless fart and barf jokes. But despite all that, the Kiddie Table is even worse.

The Kiddie Table is always an unbalanced card table, guaranteeing that someone's mashed potatoes will quickly be enjoying its new home in your lap. The tablecloth is always some plastic tarp, almost always orange and decorated with bunnies, previously used to housebreak the dog.

This tarp is used ostensibly because it easy to wash; however, this should not suggest that it has ever *been* washed. It somehow attracts sugar and starch like some kind of perverse egg-nog magnet, collecting various sticky substances until it forms a fly trap big enough to ensnare Queen Latifah.

As I've said, this table is used to separate the kids from the adults, but it never works. Parents must rush in every four seconds as their child, against every known laws of physics, somehow manages to light his fruit punch on fire.

And then there are the parents, charitably described as criminally insane traitors, who feel that *their* child should be seated next to them at the Grown-Ups Table. Apparently, they need to have their child with them because—follow *this* logic—their child lacks the motor skills to feed themselves, a trait shared by at least one of my brothers, several cousins and uncles, and one old woman whom we think is someone's great-grandmother (probably Charlemagne's), but has been around too long for any surviving descendant to remember, and no one wants to pay an anthropologist to decipher her dead language.

In any event, that means that at least one adult has to give up his seat at the Grown-Up Table and find a spot at the Kiddie Table. This was always me, despite the fact that (A) I hate children, and (B) none of those kids are mine. This puts me in an awkward position of authority, which everyone should know I can't handle. Should I stop Ricky from shoving his fork into a light socket? Eh. Let him learn like I learned.

The use of a Kiddie Table also falsely suggests that all the adults *want* to be in same room together. In fact, certain spouses should be separated immediately, so that there are no more trips to the hospital involving alcohol, a turkey slicer, and several unsightly flesh wounds.

(Admit it: Not only has this happened in your household at least once, but as your Uncle Bruce was whisked to away to the hospital with a towel wrapped around his severed fingers, you were among those who sat in the den watching *National Lampoon's Christmas Vacation.* "Hell, I ain't a doctor!" you reasoned, ironically using your mother's greatest disappointment to your sudden advantage.)

In any event, I have a career, which should be an automatic ticket to the Grown-Ups Table and put me ahead of several shiftless relatives I could mention—and *will* mention, once I get my front-row seat to all the carnage and discord that follows when thinking adults are forced into a confined space together. Plus, my fart and barf jokes will probably go over even better.

I'm done.

I HAVE A DREAM. AND IT INVOLVES CHAINSAWS.

MY GIRLFRIEND TWICE ALMOST GOT me killed. Most recently is the time she talked me into skiing, which in my case would be more accurately described as "unrestrained sliding down a hill on my ass at mach 5."

I managed not to kill myself or anyone else, though I crashed like Lindsay Lohan in a stranger's front yard after a bender. Still, I realized that it cost me $100 for two ski passes and rentals, while it would have cost me only about $2.95 for a bullet to shoot myself in the leg to avoid the humiliation.

I realize the ambulance ride would run me about $800, but I can ride in an ambulance with my dignity intact, something that's not possible when you're leaving an ass-print down the side of a hill while screaming like Howard Dean on a bad acid trip.

But this isn't the first time she almost got me killed. The first time came in a dream.

I suspect this calls for some explanation. See, it's always been my contention that it's perfectly legitimate to get angry at someone for something they did in a dream, because I feel people behave in dreams more or less how they would

25

behave in reality. As proof, I point to several of my friends who have no faces and speak in non-sequiturs. It's just their way.

I also recall a dream I had about my office being invaded by Islamic terrorists, and they were about to decapitate a female co-worker. Turns out, however, that none of the terrorists had ever chopped off a woman's head before, and none knew the proper decapitation technique. That's when a male co-worker of mine stepped up, placed the woman's head on the block, and proceeded to chop away as if he were merely slicing up some juicy celery that just happened to have long blond hair and high-pitched screams.

Now, I'm not saying that, because he killed a woman in my dream, this male co-worker had homicidal tendencies in real life. I'm just pointing out that he's always been a very helpful fellow. Plus, he's always had a low tolerance for people who don't know how to do simple tasks, such as filing alphabetically, firmly sealing envelopes, or committing bloody executions.

But back to my girlfriend's crime: I had a dream that we were on our way to a film—probably an irritating chick flick, which is a suicide hazard in itself—but she decided to stop at a salon to get her hair done. (Already, that is *so* her.) I waited for her in the lobby as she made changes to her hair—changes that I, as a male, would find imperceptible but would nonetheless have to pretend to notice, unless I want another conversation that will end with a list of my faults followed by an apology:

"How do you like my hair?" she asks.

"It's beautiful," I assure her.

"Really? What's different about it?"

"Um,…did you used to be blond?"

"No! It used to part on the right, and now it's on the

left, you insensitive bastard! How the hell could you think I was ever blond? Why don't you love me?!"

"OK, you win! I'm sorry!"

"Buy me something to make me feel better."

"How's about a Volkswagen?" That, unfortunately, is not a dream, but a nightmare I live through at least twice a week.

Anyway, here's the part of the dream where she almost killed me: As I was waiting for her to get her hair done, a man with a receding hairline entered the salon, gave me a psychotic smile, and came after me with a chainsaw.

Fortunately, that's when I woke up. And after changing the moist sheets, I knew I finally had my girlfriend at a disadvantage. Every dispute we ever had closed with my saying, "OK, you win! I'm sorry!" But this time, my girlfriend had almost gotten me killed in my dream, and it was *clearly her fault*. Obviously, she owed me an apology, and I would seek remuneration. Possibly in an unspeakable, perverted, X-rated sex act. Or possibly she'd give back my favorite shirt that she used as a bath mat six months earlier.

In any case, I raced to the phone, called my girlfriend, and told her about the guy in my dream who almost killed me because she had to get her hair done, and what do you think about that?! I settled back and waited for her apology.

Without even missing a beat, my girlfriend told me, "I had a dream that we were sledding and we crashed through the ice, and you swam to shore and left me to drown."

"OK, you win! I'm sorry!"

"Buy me a Cadillac."

How the hell do you women do this? It's bad enough you win every argument, but my girlfriend had just kicked my ass over something that *never even happened*.

Someday I hope to have a dream where I actually win

an argument with her. But because people behave in dreams they way they do in reality, I'll probably always lose. And it's for that same reason that I'll probably keep showing up at my old high school, wearing nothing but my underwear.

I'm done.

THE GREATEST FILMS
OF ALL TIME...AND WHY
THEY SUCK IT HARD

T WOULD APPEAR THAT THE TELEVISION writers' strike may cause the cancellation of this year's Oscar ceremonies, meaning that the television public will have three hours free from watching awkwardly scripted banter, unbearably cheesy musical medleys, and self-indulgent speeches thanking the gaffer from *Daddy Day Care*. Please try to limit your screams of disappointment to 90 decibels and use that extra time to do something more constructive, like, say, building a fort out all your unwatched Adam Sandler DVDs.

Perhaps you could spend that extra time reading. And if I could recommend a book at random, may I suggest *You Make a Good Point...Bonehead!* After its first year of sales, my book is rapidly approaching a benchmark, as it is a mere six copies away from reaching a dozen sales.

But sales are less important than its cultural impact. At least, that's what I try to impress upon all the book stores who are now stuck with numerous non-refundable copies that could not be given away if they came with a free bowl of soup.

Yet its cultural impact has indeed been felt by the American Film Institute. Included in my book was an essay entitled, "The Most Overrated Garbage of All Time," in which I listed several films that did not belong on the AFI's list of greatest films. Some, I felt, did not meet the standard of being "great;" others did not meet the standards of being "films," as they were clearly long, stringy strands of eel excrement.

For the record, among the films I listed were *2001, Dr. Strangelove, The Graduate, Lawrence of Arabia, Singing in the Rain, Gone with the Wind, The Godfather, Rebel Without a Cause, Some Like It Hot, Do the Right Thing*, and *Easy Rider.* As of last June, just six months after the publication of my book, *Rebel* was removed from the list, perhaps because the AFI decided that they should actually watch it and found themselves blowing chunks at the screen like a *Cloverfield* audience on a Tilt-a-whirl during a dramamine shortage.

(Curiously, some *good* films were removed as well, like *Amadeus* and *Frankenstein*, replaced with—I only wish I were kidding here—*Toy Story, Blade Runner,* and *The Sixth Sense.* Oh, yeah. An H. Night Shyamalan film made the list of greatest films ever. That ought to give you shivers the next time someone drags you to a Michael Bay film festival.)

While my original essay claimed I was done, I really wasn't. Here are some other films to avoid like Michael Medved's popcorn farts:

***Raging Bull**: I'm hardly a prude when it comes to foul language; but if you bleeped out every "f" word in this film, you'd be constantly slapping your television, trying to figure out what happened to the sound. Sure, the fights are comically violent. But if outlandish bloodletting alone equaled film greatness, the Academy would have to nominate footage of Tiger Woods and his wife.

***The Manchurian Candidate**: This was actually

dropped from AMI's list this past year, perhaps because it's about as believable as a tax tip from Wesley Snipes. It's a thinly veiled anti-Commie propaganda piece in which Frank Sinatra is brainwashed into joining an assassination plot. C'mon, brainwashed? You really think you'd have had to brainwash Sinatra to have him whack someone? All you had to do was whisper, "Hey, Frank, that guy over there said he can't tell the difference between your mother and Don Rickles' ass."

It's a Wonderful Life: First of all, let's clear something up: The only reason people watch this film is because no one bothered to renew the copyright and TV stations could run it for free. It just happened to compete for scheduling time with dead air and won, which makes it only moderately more successful than Fox Business News.

Secondly, the premise is hopelessly flawed. After all, the issue wasn't whether things would be better if Jimmy Stewart had never *existed*; the issue was whether things would be better if he dropped off that bridge like Duran Duran from the public radar. For all we know, his widow, grieving over her loss, would have given up dreams of marriage, and instead gone on to med school and later cured tuberculosis. Got a productive cough? Yeah, well, you owe it all to some wino angel! Thanks, hobo angel! Dick.

Fantasia: Hey, go figure! Pretty moving color pictures don't make classical music any less boring. This was dropped from AFI's list this past year, though it's uncertain if that was because of the film's dubious merits or the fact that Disney Studios scream "child abuse" to any parent who doesn't buy up dozens of copies for their kids, who would, in any case, get more thrills out of the *McNeil/Lehrer News Hour*.

Apocalypse Now: Naptime now. This is just a Vietnam-era update of Joseph Conrad's impenetrable novel, *Heart of Darkness*. Hey, Hollywood! If I want literature, I'll read a book! (Preferably *You Make a Good Point…Bonehead!*, available now.)

*Tootsie: Only slightly funnier than *Apocalypse Now*. I think I laughed only once at this film, and I was an easy laugh when I was eleven. Besides, there was not one moment in the film when I believed that Rudy Giuliani was a woman.

Tootsie, in fact, didn't make the AFI list but was on *Time* magazine's list. And they should at least get credit for including a comedy, since the AFI list passed on *Airplane, The Naked Gun,* and *Monty Python and the Holy Grail.* Actually, I happen to know a book that would make a great comedy. And it just so happens that I haven't sold the rights yet. But I guess I should sell the book first…

Roll credits.

MEN ARE INCESTUOUS BASTARDS

VALENTINE'S DAY IS NOW BEHIND us, which means that you men are now safe to come out from your hiding place behind the couch and re-assert yourself as the dominant member of your relationship. At least, you can do so until your girlfriend returns from the mall with your credit card and drags you to some chick flick, which will probably involve lots of crying, moaning, and weeping. And then there'll be even more of that once the film actually starts.

By now, your girlfriend has also discovered that either (a) you are a hopeless, charming romantic; or (b) you are a heterosexual male, in which case, you have the romantic sensibilities of a castrated sewer rat.

My own attempt at romance was genuine but bungled in the typical male fashion. My girlfriend hails from Honduras, so I decided to try to write her a love poem in her native tongue. One slight problem: I don't speak Spanish, other than *hola* ("hello"), *como está* ("how are you"), and *tú chupas las nalgas de monos grandes* ("you suck the buttocks of large monkeys").

This is not, shall we say, the recipe for good Valentine's Day poetry. Xmas cards, sure, but not Valentine's Day.

So I spent hours with a Spanish dictionary scribbling out a free-verse poem only to later learn something important about my girlfriend: She left Honduras at age six and therefore had no proper schooling in written Spanish. So I was writing in a language that I didn't speak and which my girlfriend couldn't read, making my poem about as intelligible as a Bob Dylan acceptance speech.

I was going to sit my girlfriend down and at least try to read what I had intended to say, but she had already called over her Spanish-speaking friend. And by "Spanish-speaking," I mean, of course, "not even remotely Spanish-speaking."

So to recap: There are now three of us at the table, trying to decipher my less-romantic-by-the-minute poem. I can't write in Spanish; my girlfriend can't read Spanish; and her friend, who was translating the poem, speaks Spanish about as well as George W. Bush speaks English.

Now, I mentioned that my Spanish was limited; but I do know this: *diosa* means "goddess." *Hermana* means "sister." These words should never, never, ever be confused, especially in the context of a love poem.

Needless to say, her friend proceeded to translate *diosa* as "female sibling." It's a bit of an understatement to say that it gave the poem an entirely different slant when, in flowery and romanticized language, she basically announced that I wanted to boff my sister.

Fortunately, her friend drained out whatever moribund romantic intent remained in my poem, as she read it with the passion of a vegetarian reading the ingredients of hot dogs. Finally, my misery came to an end when—after having declared that my sister is more beautiful than the evening star, that my sister rocks my world, and that my sister looks great naked—her friend dropped the poem like Rudy Giuliani's moist hairpiece.

At which point, my girlfriend turns to me and says, "That's really deep."

Well, yes. Declarations of incest tend to be rather heady.

In any case, it's clear that I don't really have a romantic bone in my body. Well, OK, I have *one*… (You didn't think I was too good for that old chestnut, did you?) But I think we can agree that Valentine's Day was created *for* women *by* women, although I do have an alternate theory that involves Satan.

Actually, V-Day does, in fact, have religious origins. Depending on which Christian fairy tale you believe, St. Valentine was allegedly martyred by Claudius the Cruel for either conducting illegal marriages, refusing to renounce Christianity, or for dotting his *I*'s with little hearts.

Others believe V-Day originated from the Roman festival *Lupercalia*, which translates as "The One Day A Year In Which We Prove Men Are Insensitive Scum." On that day, women would have their names drawn by lot, and their selected mate would (not joking here) whip them with animal skin, as it was believed to increase fertility. Nowadays, of course, such foreplay actually *decreases* fertility, the direct result of the man being kicked in the gonads.

The name-drawing tradition is believed to be the forerunner of the Valentine's Day card, which in turn led to many Hallmark classics like, "Be Mine," "Hold Me," and "Thank You For Not Whipping Me With A Dead Animal To Increase My Hormone Production."

One last tidbit: Some believe that the classic "heart" shape, which looks nothing like a blood-pumping muscle, was originally intended to represent a woman's bust and slender hips. Others believe that it was intended to look like a woman's butt. A little less-known fact is that the butt belonged to a young Eleanor Roosevelt, who, it was once commonly known, was a bit of slut. And, curiously, she tasted like chocolate.

I'm done.

THIS COLUMN IS NOT INTERESTING

I'VE HAD MY SHARE OF fun at my girlfriend's expense in recent months, especially with her orthodox Catholicism, a cult whose philosophy boils down to this: "Sex is icky, unless you're contributing to the overpopulation of the planet, or crushing the innocence of young altar boys."

It's also a religion that combines two of my least favorite things: (1) Pathological attachment to outdated and superstitious ceremony, culminating in the consumption of mind-altering libations and having participants collapse shaking to the floor while speaking in tongues; and (2) big, stupid hats. If I wanted to live in that kind of world, I'd move to Texas.

Her religion was particularly curious, given that she was a stripper. Granted, it was a job that she forsook after her conversion, though she told me for several weeks that "Satan was tempting" her to get back into the business of arousing creepy old men like myself.

But she would resist Satan's calling. For two months.

After which she called me and told me, "I'm going back to stripping."

"I thought you said that it was just the Devil tempting you," I said.

"Yeah," she sighed, "but I want a new car."

So there's the price of your soul, folks: A new car. The punchline to this is that she bought a Dodge Caravan. Yep. She's on the road to Hell, but at least she'll be driving a Dodge.

Some may wonder how I plan to get away with telling jokes like this about her without becoming a premature victim of the Rapture. I can joke about her because she, like virtually everyone else on the planet, has no intention of reading this column. And I know this because she described my work using the "i" word: I*nteresting*.

Now, men have come to shiver whenever their girlfriend drops the "f-bomb," which is, of course, "friends." As in, "Let's just be friends." As in, "Let's just be friends, the kind of friends who never have sex, never hang out, and never call each other, which is just as well, because if we did hang out, you'd be left squirming in your shorts wanting to bang me when all I want to do is talk about guys I'd rather have sex with more than you."

I'm never sure what else the "friends" thing is supposed to mean. It certainly doesn't mean that you can join her and her new boyfriend on their trip to her uncle's winter cabin, even if you take the trouble of hiding in their luggage. Apparently, your "friendship" extends no further than her willingness to lose your phone number while getting to keep all the stuff you gave her.

Your ex-girlfriend—excuse me, your new "friend"— also gets to keep all the stuff you intended only as loans. You know, like your money, your CD collection, your cell phone, and your hot pink lipstick. You, on the other hand, get to keep that used pair of panties that you borrowed, after convincing yourself that "borrowed" and "surreptitiously stole" are basically synonyms.

But back to the "i" word. As I said, for men, the hated "f" word is "friends." For writers, the dreaded "i" word is "interesting."

Anyone who has composed any work of art, be it a marble scale model of the Taj Mahal or their name written in feces, knows the word "interesting" is the worst insult that one can receive. "Interesting" is a hollow, vapid word, and means virtually nothing, much like the word "protection" in "President Bush's Environmental Protection Agency."

In fact, it's worse than criticism. If someone told me my writing "sucks" (and by "someone," I mean "virtually everyone"), I would at least know they're being honest with me. Telling me my writing is "interesting" is the same as saying, "Your stuff is *so* bad that, if I were to tell you my honest opinion, it would no doubt crush you like Nicole Richie caught in a bear hug between John Goodman and Roseanne Barr."

"Interesting" doesn't even have to mean "holding my interest." It can mean simply, "*of* interest," which makes your work about as significant as, say, the dog poop you just stepped into. "Interesting" can easily be applied to the greatest horrors in history, like the Hindenburg, or the Inquisition, or the Mitt Romney presidential campaign.

So when I first met my girlfriend, I provided her with—on her request, mind you—a copy of my first book, *I Hate Bush and So Do You* (a book that will be going out of print soon, partly because its lead subject will soon fade into history, but mostly because its sales suck ass).

My girlfriend called me a couple days later. "I've been reading your book."

"Oh yes?"

"It's interesting," she told me. "*Very* interesting."

And neither of us spoke of it ever again.

Interestingly enough, I'm done.

I WUZ TEACHED BY PSYKOS

LDER READERS MAY RECALL THE Rodney Dangerfield film *Back to School*, in which Rodney is confronted by the very funny and very dead comedian Sam Kinison (which is to say, he was funny then but dead now). Kinison played a college professor and Vietnam war vet that still had issues, culminating in his screaming tirade at his non-trad student Rodney, who, coincidentally, is also as dead as he was funny.

Younger viewers will recall the war veteran-slash-teacher from the MTV cartoon melodrama, *Daria*. He had a bulging eye, a perpetual growl, and a seething temper, making him the perfect comic foil. The point is, the "war veteran as psycho teacher" stereotype has proven time and time again that nothing screams comedy like post-traumatic stress disorder, much in the same way that *Hogan's Heroes* brought us the hilarity of Nazi prison camps.

And, like every stereotype, it is 100% true. At least, it was certainly true of my 6th grade teacher, who, if carbon dating is to be believed, was a veteran of the Korean War. He had a lot of pet peeves, including pencils that were too short (they had to be as long as your pinkie or thrown out), improperly folded papers, sloppy handwriting, and pupils who observed—in his own best interest, mind you—that he just might be an anal-retentive psycho.

On one memorable day, his primary concern was that we students weren't following instructions. "I'd like to tell you a funny story," he began, indicating to us in advance that what would follow would be about as funny as a drowning puppy, a root canal, or an early Johnathon Winters album. Or, worse, a later Johnathon Winters album.

"Here's a funny story about a guy who wouldn't listen," he continued. "The sergeant in my platoon warned us about peeking over the top of our trench. But there was one soldier who *didn't listen*. He looked over the top of the trench and—BAM! A sniper got 'im right between the eyes! Now do you think that's a funny story?! Do you?! Do you think that's a *funny story*?!"

"Actually, no," I said. "Maybe it's your timing."

Okay, I didn't really say that. Would you have made a smartass remark to someone who thinks a guy getting shot in the head is a funny story? I didn't think so.

Now, let me stress that I think all junior-high teachers should be eligible for combat pay. They have one of the most difficult, most underappreciated, most crap-taking job this side of a newspaper columnist. But while I am willing to cut some slack to most of my former teachers, there are some who are not cut out for speaking to children, much less teaching them; and we all would've been better off if they had gone with their first choices of profession, be it a prison guard, a bar bouncer, or a professional dogfighter.

For example, in my latest book, *You Make a Good Point… Bonehead!*, I discuss my junior-high home-ec teacher, whom I affectionately refer to as "Miss Pigface." This was not her real name, even though, had her parents in fact named her "Pigface," it would have revealed a staggering amount of prescience on their parts. (Incidentally, this is not a plug for my book, although it is available at Amazon, and you must purchase it now now NOW!)

Equally terrifying in his own way was my shop teacher, whom I shall refer to as "Dick Assface." Again, that's not his name, although conversations about him during lunch period suggested otherwise. Much like my Korean vet teacher, Mr. Assface had his own pet peeves, which included students, other faculty, and the existence of other people on the planet.

The first day began thusly: Dick wrote his name on the chalkboard and proceeded to bitch about it. "That's how you spell my name!" he barked bitterly. "I didn't realize that there were so many ways to spell it, but *people* keep asking me how to spell it, so I keep having to write it on the board!"

My, will the horrors ever cease? First of all, if you think there's only one way to spell someone's name, can we agree that you shouldn't be teaching in public schools? There are plenty of ways to spell people's names in this country—just ask Tiphani and Caerin. I could easily think of other ways to spell his name. My own name could be spelled "Johnson" or "Jonson" or "Johnsen." Even a common name like Smith could be spelled "Smith" or "Smyth" or even "Smythe," in some uptight, fancy-pants circles. And "Dick Assface" could be "Dik Assphase" or something. The only person who wouldn't know that is a dick or an assface, or perhaps some shop-teaching hybrid of the two.

He was retiring that year, and my class bore the brunt of his "screw-it-I'm-leaving-soon-anyway" attitude, as he unloaded more of his demons than a shop teacher with all ten fingers had a right to have. As far as I know, he retired, died, and brought joy to other people only when I had the pleasure of whizzing on his grave.

Now isn't that a funny story?

I'm done.

GOT ANAL WART CREAM?

Part One: The part where I need anal wart cream

THE BEST THING ABOUT SHOPPING on the Internet is the convenience: Just log on, click, and you've got that rare LP copy of *Jim Nabor's Greatest Polka Hits*. And best of all, you can get it without having the sales clerk laughing in your pathetic face.

Online shopping gets a little less convenient, however, if you've ever shopped at an business that I'll call incompetentmoronsfromhell.com. In the interest of protecting this paper from a libel suit, I don't want to say exactly what company I dealt with on this particular occasion. I will say only that it was a *drugstore* with a *dot com* address.

Considering the large number of customer service representatives (or, to use the more technical term, "clerks") that I would eventually deal with, it was fortunate that I was not purchasing anything particularly embarrassing: It was just the usual pharmaceutical cocktail I use to control my incontinence, itchy scrotum, and anal warts.

I assure readers that I was buying this over the Internet simply for the convenience, and not because I have any shame. Only lesser men would feel any compunction about letting the college-age checkout girl know that he wets himself while scratching his privates and clutching his buttcheeks. It happens to all of us, as does the extra-loud price check over the store intercom, which I believe was originally designed to screech fire alerts to residents of rural Argentina.

Anyway, I placed my order with this online drugstore, and even added an additional purchase of scrotum dye, to change the color back from green to a more sociably acceptable pink.

Soon after my online purchase, I received an email that read: "We regret to inform you that there will be a short delay in your order. We apologize for the inconvenience, and we will ship your order as soon as possible."

Now, when I read "short delay," I assumed that this meant—and I admit the fault is totally mine here—that the delay would be short. I decided that I could tough it out just a couple more days, even if it meant a few more days of pee-stained underwear and rainbow-colored testicles.

Seven weeks later, the situation in my pants was becoming, shall we say, a tad untenable.

I decided it was time to contact customer service. I emailed them with my order number and asked, in my usual restrained manner, that I expected either (1) my order to arrive in the next five seconds; (2) a full refund; or (3) a customer service representative to arrive at my house and personally scratch my balls for me.

Needless to say, they disregarded the last two options. I got a cheerful email back from customer service, saying that, if I wanted to call their 1-800 number, they would happily expedite my order.

Well. If I wanted to phone in my order, I would have done that seven weeks earlier. The whole point of ordering online is that I wouldn't have to deal with the labyrinth that is the Selection Menu of No Return: "If you are in the United States, press 1. If you want useless automated information that you already know, press 2. If you want to hear the same useless crap all over again, press 3. And if you are using a rotary phone, press 4 on your keypad."

Personally, I'd rather pluck my anal warts out with a tweezer. Unfortunately, I'd probably have to buy the tweezer in person, and I wouldn't want anyone at the store to think I pluck my *eyebrows*. ("No, seriously, I'm just using it to pull out my anal warts!" "Thanks, dude, but I'm just the stockboy.")

Anyway, I figured that the reason for the "short" seven-week delay was the inordinately large amount of anal wart cream I ordered, and they probably had to wait a few weeks for the extra crates to ship from Bangkok. It sounded like a reasonable explanation. Seriously: My rectum has more cream than an 8-track tape of 1970s-era love songs.

So I decided, what the heck, I'll just cancel the order and re-order a few minutes later, figuring out that, by that time, they ought to have anal wart cream coming out of their buttholes. So to speak.

Part Two: Seriously, I'll pay you. I got money.

So to summarize the story so far: an online retailer told announced a "short delay" in my order, which was now seven weeks and counting. There was also a great car chase, some really neat explosions, and hot love scene with me and big-butt model Vida Guerra.

And was Vida turned off by my incontinence, itchy scrotum, and anal warts? She was so totally *not* repulsed. Seriously, it scared even me.

After seven weeks of hilarious jokes about my yellowed underpants, flaky ball skin, and flaming rectum, I decided to cancel my order and get my money back. I logged back on to their website, incompetentmoronsfromhell.com.

(Again, that's not their real name, although it would be more in line with the FDA's "truth in advertising" clause. Incidentally, I'd like to apologize to any incompetent morons from hell that I may have offended by using their website's name, unless, of course, it's a website owned by the Sen. Norm Coleman campaign.)

Anyway, as I tried to cancel my order online, I received an automated message: "Our system has detected that you are using an AOL account. Because of this, we are unable to forward you to our customer help desk."

Well! This seemed a little peculiar, as I'd been using an AOL account to place my initial order. Yet, for some strange reason, canceling my order could not be done the same way. Why would a company make canceling an order more difficult that placing one? Who can say? The mysteries of Internet commerce are vast, indeed.

Fortunately, to prove that they still wanted to be helpful, they provided me with a link to their Customer Help form. I filled it out, including my name, my email address, my order number, and the types of colors my balls had turned in the time it took to fill out the form.

Then I clicked Enter. And I got back a giant red error message that read, "Error: The email address you provided is already registered with us."

I'd like to repeat that, this time using gratuitous capitalization: I COULDN'T GET CUSTOMER SERVICE BECAUSE I WAS ALREADY A CUSTOMER. Apparently, their computers were not designed to deal with repeat customers, and it confused their systems in a way that Y2K and East Indian pranksters never could.

I had to send my cancellation request via a different email address—which fortunately I had, due to a complex scheme to hide from my girlfriend all my Internet footprints to the anal-wart specialist sites.

So I filled out the cancellation request again, this time using my Juno email account instead of the AOL account that had caused the initial snafu. I included my name and order number again, so only a pea-brained rodent could mess it up.

It was at this point that they again messed it up. I got back a message saying, "We cannot cancel this order because the order number does not match any email address we have on file."

Well! Let's summarize: (1) they can't cancel an order from anything other than my original AOL account; (2) they can't process a request made from an AOL account; and (3) Customer Service is unavailable if you're already a registered customer; and (4) enjoy your free copy of *Catch-22*.

Naturally, I wrote back and told them of the conundrum they had caused. And then I added, with my typical tactfulness, that they were the biggest sack of retards I'd seen outside the Bush Justice Department, and could they all suck on my pus-oozing boils, get incurable brain cancer, and die die die *die*?! Granted, that last part may have been my seven-week-old anal warts talking.

Finally, yet another customer service representative (read, "overpaid intern") wrote back and told me that I could cancel my order in one of two ways: (1) I could cancel the order through my original email account; or (2) I could cancel through my current email simply by sending them the account number.

Well! I wrote back yet again, explaining that: (1) no, I cannot cancel the order on my original email; and in any case, (2) this is what I've been trying to do for the past week; and (3) seriously, you should really get down and blow me so that my untreated incontinence allows me to piss down your lying, moronic throat. At this point, it was just *me* talking.

So finally—*finally*—I received a refund for my undelivered drugs. However, by that time, I had already treated my anal warts with some cool hair-styling gel and my incontinence with some well-placed duct tape. My itchy balls were also no longer a problem, due largely to the fact that they had long since dropped off and rolled under the sink.

But in the end, I had learned a valuable lesson: Employees at online drug stores are scarfing down their own merchandise. Actually, I kind of hope they're enjoying my anal wart cream, as well. At least I know they'll be getting something right up the butt.

At last, I'm done.

TRY ABSTINENCE! NOW WITH A 20-30% SUCCESS RATE!

WE'VE NOW BLOWN ANOTHER $1.3 billion on abstinence-only sex-ed curriculum to find that, lo and behold, teens are still horny. Worse, 70 to 80 percent of teens who go through the abstinence-only courses eventually engage in unprotected sex. And about 30 percent of those have it with R. Kelly.

Look, abstinence didn't work for the Spears' kids, and it won't work for yours, either. One day they'll be proclaiming their chastity, and the next they'll be married to their high school crush in a Vegas wedding officiated by an Elvis impersonator, who, ironically, will be the only one using the Pill.

It's not as though abstinence teachers are unwilling to teach about birth control. For example, they love to cite stats about the failure rates of condoms, or perpetuate the myth that abortion causes breast cancer—a claim also made by the state-controlled health website run under the aegis of Republican governor Tim Pawlenty. Fortunately, critics got Pawlenty to retract that "abortion-leads-to-cancer" claim, but only in a backhanded manner, after Pawlenty only begrudgingly admitted that "skankiness" is not a form of cancer.

Of course, all the talk about contraception failure—the percentage of which is far lower than the failure rate of abstinence courses—merely persuade the kids to go without contraception altogether, apparently resorting to just thinking about baseball. And by "baseball," I mean, "NY Yankee Johnny Damon banging his ridiculously hot swimsuit model wife Michelle in center field."

What staggers me the most about abstinence-only crowd is not just their refusal to acknowledge the *failure* of these programs, but the *results* of them even if they were successful. A kid who waits until marriage to have sex almost guarantees that, upon graduation from high school, he'll marry the first dope who says yes—most likely another "abstinent" teen—only to find that he's married a serial killer with daddy issues and an uncomfortable knowledge of rare, untraceable poisons. Even worse, she gets fat.

Besides, I'm 37 and I've never been married. Do you think I planned to wait until marriage to have sex? I couldn't even wait until the end of third period math class.

Fine, I'm lying. I was abstinent myself through high school. Of course, in my day, we had another name for abstinent teens: UGLY. Yeah, the teens not having sex? Those were pretty much just the ugly teens. You don't need a "purity ring" when you have "loser stink."

Try talking to an abstinent teen, and you'll see the future of rooftop shooters:

"Oh no I'm not a loser why do you say I'm a loser I'm just abstinent!"

"Why are you shaking so much?"

"I'm just so excited about being abstinent oh my god is that a doughnut I gotta fuck it!"

Now, I may sound harsh on us ugly kids, but I'm not the only one. You may notice that when a kid goes missing on the cable news networks, it's always a cute kid, generally white, from a wealthy background. This often prompts the PC crowd to ask, "Oh, and I suppose it would be less tragic if the kid was ugly?"

Well, let me think for a min—YES.

Hell, it's *far* less tragic when the kid is ugly. You know why? Because things are more valuable when they're rare. If gold were as plentiful as ugly kids, gold would be worthless. That's why missing cute kids make the news and kids who look like my first-grade self do not.

It's also why there are headlines like, "Armed robbers made off with half a million dollars in cash and jewelry," and not, "Armed robbers made off with four bags of dog turds." Nobody cares, not even the people who own the dog turds. They'll just make more.

And that's how ugly kids' parents should react, too. Their kid goes missing, and they tell the press, "Ah, we'll be fine. I'll just have some really gross sex with my hideous pig-faced wife and we'll pump out another one even uglier than the last. There's no shortage of ugly bullets in this veiny, purple stun gun!"

Incidentally, if you're a parent and you don't agree with me that ugly kids are worth less than attractive kids, I've got news for you: Your child is abstinent.

I'm done.

WE, THE MEDIA ELITE: YOU OWE US YOUR PATHETIC LIVES!

REALIZE THE FOLKS AT MSNBC lost a good friend when Tim Russert passed, and a certain amount of televised tributes were inevitable. But after their 96-hour solid "Remembering Russert" marathon, followed by another week of hourly "Remembering Russert" updates, I began to pray for the journalistic detachment that the media usually reserve for stories about illegal wiretapping and naked-men pyramids.

Yes, I know it's tacky telling the deceased friends how to grieve. But I wonder if Russert's memory was well-served by such poor editorial judgement. It took less time for the public to absorb the Pope's death, or Reagan's. That kind of non-stop coverage should be reserved solely for the Anna Nicole Smiths of the world.

That said, it's my turn to remember Tim Russert.

Russert had a way of nailing politicians with their own words, something Sen. Joe Biden learned when he appeared on the show in 2007. Biden had just caught flak for calling Obama "articulate and clean," which sounded as if he were surprised that a black man could talk and bathe. Biden quickly put that to rest:

Biden: When I said he was "clean," what I meant is that he's "fresh."

Russert: By "fresh," you mean Obama's like a watermelon?

B: No! Not like a watermelon! No, I just mean Obama brings something new to the table.

R: So Obama's your manservant.

B: Dear God, no! I'm just saying he's made a remarkable climb to the top of the political heap.

R: So Obama's a monkey?

B: Nooooo! I just mean he's captured the hearts and minds of the American people!

R: So he steals things?

B: *Nooooo!* Look, let me be very clear: Barack Obama has the prescription to cure what's wrong with this country.

R: So he deals drugs?

B: *Argh!* He's a man of great style!

R: So he's gay?

B: *Bite me, honkey*! I'm not digging this jive turkey!

Yes, that's correct: Joe Biden speaks black circa 1972.

Of course, Russert didn't usually have to finagle someone into saying something stupid. More recently, Russert asked senior Hillary Clinton advisor Terry McAuliffe why Clinton was still in the race at that point, having no chance to overtake Obama in the delegate count. McAuliffe referenced Russert's father, Big Russ, saying that Terry's dad and Big Russ were "probably both in heaven right now, Tim, probably having a scotch, looking down and saying, you know what, this fight goes on."

Which was a tad bit awkward, of course, because Russert's dad is alive and well, unlike McAuliffe's credibility.

Russert pointed that his dad was, in fact, watching the show in the green room, prompting McAuliffe to ask, "Um, are you sure? Have you checked up on him during the commercial break? Cuz I just playfully hit him over the head with a shovel and he wasn't moving then." He then tried to make amends to Russert by offering to store the body in the cooler from his minivan but became defensive when Russert asked to remove the smoked sausages.

Again, I don't mean to diminish Russert's accomplishments, but the media do tend to exaggerate their own importance, as I've clearly stated before in this column—which, by the way, is the only thing that is currently keeping the terrorists at bay, California still attached to the mainland, and the Lohans from producing another kid.

When ABC talked about replacing Ted Koppel's *Nightline* with David Letterman's *Late Night*, Koppel produced an ad insinuating that his show is "more important than ever" in the age of terrorism. So that's what's been preventing the next 9/11— What? Koppel's been off the air for almost three years? Well, I guess Koppel kept the homeland secure about as well as Stupid Pet Tricks.

Perhaps I'm just jealous because no one will be having week-long tributes to me when I croak. Although I could envision week-long arguments about who's going to pay all those public urination fines.

I'm done.

O SAY CAN YOU SEE THAT OUR NATIONAL ANTHEM IS LAME?

KNOW THIS WILL NEVER GET me elected in Detroit; but compared to Japanese cars, American cars suck more than an Asian whore. I've driven two American cars, and both spent more time on the repairman's rack than on the road. Meanwhile, my Nissan, with 200K-plus miles on it, continues to sputter on, surprising everyone that it hasn't died yet, not unlike a four-wheeled Bob Dole but with better treads.

This admission will no doubt receive accusations of anti-Americanism, which is ridiculous, because we liberals are already known for hating America. Hell, we just nominated a radical Muslim terrorist for president.

No, I'm kidding, of course. Obama is, in fact, a radical Buddhist terrorist. But I'm not joking about the suckiness of American cars, which, despite having several brand names like Ford or Chevy, were all, in fact, produced by Tonka. Japanese cars, by contrast, are built to last. And let's face it, they have to be, if they have any chance of out-running Godzilla.

And that's the real reason Japanese cars are better: It's

not because Americans are lazy and apathetic; it's because we don't have Godzilla. We have Newt Gingrich, but it's not quite the same. And, of course, Americans are lazy and apathetic, as clearly evidenced by the preponderance of reality shows.

Over the recent 4th of July holiday, during a time when we should be reflecting on the grand freedoms endowed to us by our creators—and then immediately removed by Bush's new FISA law—I was struck by another unpleasant revelation: "The Star-Spangled Banner" is one lame national anthem.

Yes, I realize that pointing this out merely solidifies the right wing's view of liberals as unpatriotic terrorist-huggers, even after I repeatedly assure them that my life-size poster of Mahmoud Ahmadinejad, currently taking up 4' 6" of wall space in my bedroom, has nothing to do with politics, and everything to do with his being a healthy-bearded chunk of dictatorial man-meat.

Nevertheless, it must be said: Our national anthem is lame. Here are the main reasons, and you'll note that none of them have to do with hating my country, and certainly not the fine, outstanding FBI men who, thanks to FISA, are now reading my emails:

(1) "The Star-Spangled Banner" is stolen from the British. Specifically, this was an old drinking song, "To Anacreon in Heaven," by redcoat composer John Stafford Smith. I know, this seems petty to mention, especially after England has become our ally and gave us Benny Hill, The Beatles, and plenty of giggles over things like "spotted dick."

But seriously: We fought a war to get away from this people! We changed "theatre" to "theater" and "favour" to "favor," but we kept their ale-guzzling chanty as our freakin' national anthem?! We might as well adopt Iraq's national anthem as our own, although it may be tough to get sports stadiums to rise for lyrics like: "Death to America / Death to America / Foxy baby let me touch your veil / Then bring death to America, oh yeah."

And don't write me and tell me those aren't the lyrics to the Iraqi national anthem. What they really say and how it's been translated are two different things. Sure, it may sound like your cab driver is saying, "Thank you for your generous $1 tip," but he's actually comparing your mother to something left behind by a camel.

(2) Nobody can sing our anthem. OK, almost nobody other than a professional choir singer with vocal chords more flexible than a boneless spider-monkey. The song has those ridiculously low notes—the kind that are uncomfortably close to the ones that make people fudge their undies—and then soon jump three octaves higher and can be reached only by giving oneself a healthy testicular tug.

(3) No one can remember the words. In fact, a history teacher of mine conducted an experiment to see how many kids in our class could write out its lyrics. Almost no one got them totally correct, and only one girl could correctly identify the word "donserly." If you don't know what "donserly" is, you're clearly stupid, because it's right there in the first line: "O say can you see, by the donserly light." I believe "donserly" is defined as, "pertaining to light that one O can see."

(I honestly don't recall how well I did transcribing our anthem's lyrics. Like most students, I suspect I did not get them fully correct either, as my mind was hard-wired into remembering only the most critical of details, such as the precise minute the cheerleaders would be leaving the girls' locker room.)

(4) It's bad poetry. If I submitted this to my college writing teacher, I probably would have failed for the changing rhyme scheme alone. But even if it were good poetry, it clearly doesn't belong to this music: The words had to be contorted and contracted to fit the British melody, and they fit as well as Kirstie Alley in ballerina tights.

This is why we get awkward words like "o'er," as in "o'er the ramparts we watched," and "o'er the land of the free." It's not even a real word: Who the hell says "o'er" for "over"? Was anyone, anytime in history, ever that pressed for time? It makes us sound like a nation of speech impediments, as if Bush didn't do that every time he mentions "ter'rists."

And as for the other three verses— What? You didn't know there *were* three other verses? It's probably just as well: I won't dissect all of them, except to say that there's a reason we don't sing them. They're unbelievably bad, totally unsingable, and grossly over-use the word "zesty."

Here's just one line from verse three, referring to the British occupiers: "Their blood has wash'd out their foul footsteps' pollution." I mean…holy fucking goddamned shit. Kind of makes that whole Toby Keith "boot up your ass" song look like a gay valentine from Dan Fogelberg.

Does "The Star-Spangled Banner" have *anything* going for it? Well, sure, maybe that last stanza is kind of catchy. And maybe whenever I hear it played right, it makes me bawl like Spike Lee after a negative film review. Of course, if you tell anyone I said that, I'll run o'er you with my Nissan.

I'm done.

MY DAD THROWS PUKE
BETTER THAN YOUR DAD!

IT WAS MY FATHER'S BIRTHDAY recently, and once again I got him the same gift I gave him for Father's Day: a box of diddly squat, minus the box. I also gave him the contents of Brooke Hogan's head, plus a gift certificate made out to one Mr. Jack Shit.

This is my snarky way of saying that I got my dad a bowlful of the imaginary cereal, Zippy Nada Crunchy Nothingness. I got him a big box of zen.

Some would say this makes me a lousy son. And some should mind their own damn business, as I don't recall asking for some's opinion. Besides, it doesn't make me a lousy son. My criminally insane attraction to arson already has that covered.

But I at least tell my father I love him, right? Ha ha ha! Don't be silly. I am a man; and as all men know, telling another man you love him is really, really gay. Even if that man is someone who sacrificed his life's dreams and much of his annual salary to raise his son to be successful, and that son winds up being a shiftless, underemployed genetic dead end, whose biggest success was procuring a 27,172 customer-reviewer rank on Amazon.com.

Still, like most people, I believe my father to be the

greatest ever. But rather than say so directly, I will have to illustrate my father's greatness in a way that befits my manly position: an anecdote filled with barf jokes.

I was young and attending a family reunion in Iowa, neither condition I would recommend to anyone. I was perhaps as young as eight, or as old as twelve; I really don't recall. Suffice it to say that I was young enough to be sexually appealing to Michael Jackson.

For those who have never attended a family reunion, it goes something like this: You drive for hundreds of miles, collecting various odors in the back seat and spending nights in motels that were clearly designed solely to trap roaches, only to arrive at your destination and spend a couple days talking with relatives that you are already sick of, because they lived three blocks from your home.

Naturally, as a kid in Iowa, there was little to do around the adults, especially as I didn't care for the taste of beer. So I spent the days ingesting the typical young boy's diet, which consists of Coke and Pop Rocks.

We spent the night at the home of a woman whom we barely knew, and I retired to bed (and by "bed," I of course mean "a pillow and blanket on the floor"), without memorizing a critical detail: the path to the toilet. It was a lapse in memory that I would come to regret, but apparently not learn from.

Some time past midnight, the Coke and Pop Rocks began seeking a prompt exit from my body through the most convenient hole in my body, which, as it turned out, was not my asshole. Apparently the Coke/Pop Rocks mixture was too high-strung to be bothered with navigating the miles of my intestinal tract and decided instead to exit from the entrance door.

Of course, it was dark, I was in an unfamiliar house, and I was, to say the least, pressed for time. I staggered around the house, managing to find the bathroom but not the light switch. No time. I reached out with my hand, put my hand on a porcelain object I guessed to be a sink, and—

Blearghhh!

It was then I learned an important life lesson, one that every young man must know in order to become a man: When you puke Coke and Pop Rocks, it glows in the dark.

I can't tell you how cool this is. Part of me was suffering, thinking, "Man, am I really sick!" And the other part was saying, "I just discovered King Solomon's mines!"

But while I felt much better, there was a slight problem. You know how peanut butter has no "chunky" style? It has "creamy," and it has "super chunk." My vomit happened to be in the category of "super-duper, gum-tearing, scraping-enamel-off-the-teeth" chunky. Also known as the "no way are you going to wash this down the sink"chunky.

After several attempts by both my father and me to wash the offending substance down the drain, my father did what I'm sure any of you readers would do for me: He reached in the sink, grabbed a fistful of puke, and began tossing it in the toilet by hand.

Now, this alone would make my father the greatest dad in the world. But that's not the end of the story.

As I said, in at least 30 years, I've not gotten my father a present for his birthday or Father's Day. And for 30 years straight, my father did not turn to me and say, "You didn't get me anything? No, that's all right. After all, it's not like *I fished your puke out of the sink with my bare hands or anything.*"

And that's why he's the greatest dad ever.

I'm done.

REVENGE IS BEST SERVED WITH A BOOT TO THE HEAD

ENCOUNTERED A OLD CLASSMATE OF mine on MySpace and requested that I be added to her friends' list, figuring that she couldn't possibly still be angry with me because of our freshman year in high school, 22 years ago, when I gave her the nickname "Lizard."

After a couple of days of no response, I logged into her MySpace page to see if she had received my request, only to get the message: "This account has been set to Private."

Oh, yeah. Still pissed about that lizard thing.

I suspect she experienced a failure to translate Dude language into Chick. Consider these statements to different subjects:

Dude #1 to Dude #2: "Hey, you stinky douchebag!"

Naturally, Dude #2 hears: "You are a valued friend. I enjoy your company so much that, if you do smell bad, it is not so offensive as to jeopardize our friendship. I also do not judge harshly your hobby of cleansing women's hidey-holes. In fact, I envy it."

Now consider this exchange:

Dude #1 to Chick: "Hey, lizard!"

Chick hears: "You are a lizard."

Chick then thinks, "He shall pay for that, if I have to

wait 22 years, by which time we shall be using an alternate form of communication, perhaps by denying him the number of the video-phone in my lunar pod."

Of course, I'm hardly one to condemn another for holding a grudge. I still hate my entire 2nd grade class, all of whom I pray one day to see in the Obits page after a fatal accident involving slippery pavement and a steamroller.

Their crime? Around Halloween, we were asked to draw a holiday-themed picture which would then be voted on by other students. Now, lest I be accused of false modesty, let me say that *clearly* my picture was the *best in the class.*

It had a haunted house with goblins and ghosts peering out the windows, a witch flying overhead, a bat flying past the moon, and even some creepy hand sticking out of the manhole in front. What horror! What pathos! And this was during the '70s, a time in which audiences were difficult to creep out, as evidenced by the fact that Sonny and Cher warranted a prime-time TV show with no parental guidance suggested.

Anyway, as you might suspect, my Halloween picture got exactly one vote: mine. It would be something I would painfully recall on my prom night, after losing the vote for Homecoming Queen to some lizard-looking chick.

To make matters worse, I tied with the "slow kid" in the class. By "slow kid," I don't mean he was officially mentally retarded. He was what experts would today call "learning disabled," or "developmentally challenged." Or, to put it in medical terms, "in serious need of smarty pills."

Yet, indeed, I tied with Slow Kid, even though I had drawn a creepy haunted house with a bucketful of colorful characters, and he drew a freakin' jack-o-lantern. All he drew was a jagged-line mouth and triangle-shaped eyes on a circle, one that wasn't remotely circular but looked more butt-shaped, with the left buttock suffering from a serious case of gigantism.

Then he colored it orange. By "colored," I mean he obviously fired an orange-crayon-colored paintball at it, hoping that it would splatter across the jagged-mouthed butt image he drew, but apparently unconcerned if he missed the page entirely and colored his entire desktop orange, a trait I had long chalked up to his inability to properly consume Cheetos.

Yet, despite the odds against it, at least some of the orange color made it inside the lines of the pumpkin. And with that, he was able to achieve a tie-vote with my phatasm-agoric masterpiece. He was able to equal me with just one orange crayon, a butt-shaped dream, and a roomful of little 2nd-grade buttheads, who perhaps saw themselves in the drawing.

Worse yet, I don't even think that even Slow Kid voted for himself. I don't think he was smart enough to realize he *could* vote for himself. This means that someone voted for him out of pity. And that's what really hurts: the realization that, in the 2nd-grade Halloween picture election of '78, I was tied with a young Ralph Nader.

But if I ever encounter my heathen classmates again, I would never do something so passive-aggressive as to shut off access to my MySpace page. Rather, if violence is not an option, I'll be reduced to my usual retort: calling them stinky douchebags.

I'm done.

I HATE SARAH PALIN
AND SO DOES JESUS

T TICKED ME OFF TO hear that Jerry Lewis had another record year with his Telethon. Personally, I say to Hell with Jerry's Kids. Seriously, how many thousands of kids does Lewis have, and why do they all have the same fucking disease? What are the odds?

Stop having kids, Jerry Lewis! There's obviously something wrong with your gene pool. And we're tired of picking up the tab. Forget the Telethon—here's a quarter for a condom. Use the change to buy yourself a new hairpiece.

Ironically, I have an ally in Sarah Palin, who sneers at such community activism. "I guess being a small-town mayor is sort of like a community organizer," she said in her acceptance speech in St. Paul, "except a mayor has actual responsibilities."

You go, girl. Only a small-town mayor could be responsible enough to fire a librarian for not burning all the books.

Knowing that Palin is a fundamentalist Christian, I emailed a reverend buddy of mine to help me wrestle with a nagging question I had. "Wasn't Jesus supposedly a community activist?" I asked.

"Yes," he said. "And you know who was a governor? *Pontius Pilate.*"

Yeah, I guess Pontius Pilate is sort of like a small-town mayor. Except he didn't do nearly as much to damage Christianity.

But Palin's Christ-loathing didn't stop there: "And what does he hope to accomplish," she asked of Senator Barack Obama, "after *turning back the waters* and *healing the planet*?"

Geez, I dunno, but who gives a rat's ass? That would still be an impressive first week in office. In fact, I don't think I'd even need a follow-up act. If you're still not impressed with a guy who can turn back floods and cure global warming, I humbly suggest that you may be setting the bar a tad too high. ("What are you going to do next, President Obama? Lead?!")

Hell, for all I care, Obama could do freakin' card tricks for the rest of his term: "No, Mr. President, it's not the ace of spades. But hey, ace of spades, three of diamonds, whatever. Remember when you turned back that hurricane with your hands? That was *awesome!*"

And if I'm reading Palin's argument correctly, she seems to be arguing that we shouldn't vote for Obama because… he's *miraculous.* So to be clear, Palin doesn't like miracles, and she doesn't like community activists, which can mean only one thing: Palin—an evolution-denying, Rapture-awaiting Christian—absolutely hates Jesus.

Which actually makes some kind of sense, because— let's face it—Jesus would hate this bitch, too. And if Palin really *did* speak for Jesus, we'd be forced to ask ourselves: Exactly at what point in the last 2000 years did Jesus become a big dick?

Sure, 2000 years is a long time for one to hold the same philosophy and values. Let's look at this in perspective: Thirty years ago, my favorite song was "Rhinestone Cowboy." So

I suppose it's possible that Jesus underwent some massive re-evaluation in the past two millenia:

Disciple: "But Jesus, didn't you say, 'Thou shallt not steal'?"

Jesus: "My child—my dear, moronic child—that was *so* before plasma television. Now climb through the window and hand me the set, will ya?"

Disciple: "What makes you think the window will be open?"

Jesus: "It will be open! Ala-KAZAMM!"

[Note to offended Christians: I of course am being ironic when I suggest that Jesus would yell "kazamm" before using his sorcerous powers to steal a plasma TV. I'm sure he would just say "Amen."]

Much has been said about Palin's joke-telling ability, though I have to wonder if she forgets the punchlines: "What's the difference between a hockey mom and a pitbull?" she asks.

Wait, wait, let me guess! Three IQ points? The pitbull has a conscience? Pitbulls are less hairy? Pitbulls believe in man-made climate change? I'd rather fuck the pitbull?

"Lipstick!"

Oh, right, lipstick! At least a pitbull has the decency to wear makeup while it's humping Exxon Mobil's leg. Although it says a lot about the new VP candidate when Obama said, "You can't put lipstick on a pig," and Republicans immediately thought he was talking about Palin.

By the way, if I may address Gov. Palin personally—and I know she's reading this paper, because, as she confessed to Katie Couric, she reads *all* newspapers—let me just add this: Governor, stop claiming that you represent "small-town America." I *come* from a small town, and I think you're a dumb hick.

Amen.

WHO'S A GUY GOTTA FUCK TO GET FUCKED IN THIS TOWN?!

THE COLD REALITY IS THAT, no matter how hard parents try to keep kids from finding porn on the Internet, kids are going to find porn. It doesn't matter if you use filters, child locks, or an overweight nanny sitting on the keyboard.

This is because everything you search for on the web leads to porn. Sports statistics? Porn. The Gettysburg Address? Porn. Recipes for melons and wieners? Porn. Reconfigured tax levies on capital gains and eligible dividends? Holy crap, you are looking at some hardcore, mathematically erotic and incomprehensible porn. With lots of big, round numbers.

But I've learned that one can really find porn if—as is the case with me—one is looking for porn.

During my porn search, I came across a picture of a woman who looked uncannily like my favorite Playboy model, Carmella DeCesare. But this wasn't 2004's Playmate of the Year, oh no. This woman was an "escort"—by which I mean she followed you to your car at night to make sure you were safe in the parking lot.

And then she would escort you to a cheap motel and escort you to an orgasm.

Best of all: This goddess was located in the Twin Cities. A Carmella DeCesare lookalike is in the *same state as I am.* That fact alone was enough to get me pointing to the North Star, if you catch my drift.

She was, of course, way out of my price range, which is exactly how it should be. One does not feed angus beef steaks to hoboes. Fine cuts of meat like this are reserved solely for Eliot Spitzer.

The rest of us plebeians must be content to feed on the scraps from Duluth's harbor side, scraps that don't require condom usage, mainly because their happy-traps have, through years of abuse and overuse, developed an impenetrable layer of scales.

[Note to any law enforcement agency reading this: Obviously I would not, in any case, attempt to contact this "escort" for the totally immoral purpose of having consensual adult sex. But for the record, to merely share breathing space with a Carmella DeCesare lookalike, I'd be willing to break state, national, and intergalactic law, as well as take Gallagher's mallet to my left nut. After that nut had been properly utilized, of course.]

I did, in fact, wind up contacting the woman, but only to ask what I thought was a legitimate question about her ad. Her escort service ad contained this line, and I must assure readers that this is 100% true: "Available for weddings."

I felt this needed some slight clarification. "What does it mean that you are available for weddings?" I wrote to her. "You mean, like, during the ceremony? Doesn't that piss off the bride? Is the man required to love, honor, obey, and to not be a cop?"

Surprisingly, as legitimate as these questions are, I never got a response. All I can say to guys is this: If you find a girlfriend who is willing to say "I do" while you're ejaculating on a hooker's stomach, marry your girlfriend *now*. You have what we bachelors call "a keeper."

I also happened to find a VIP escort who was based here in Duluth. I wasn't able to email her questions, though, because the only way to contact her was by filling out a Client Background Check, which—it should come as no surprise to anyone reading this—I would not have a chance in hell of passing.

That was fine, though, because I saw enough of the woman's website to determine that this particular escort was almost as old as I am. And if I wanted to have sex with a woman my age, I would, well, *have sex with a woman my age*. I'd simply wait at the Medicine Shoppe for some sexy widow grandma to pick up her arthritis medicine on her way to the Bingo hall and...*Bingo*!

I pity any fellow looking for by-the-hour love in this podunk town. Not that I would know: Who has time for actual human contact with all this porn to sift through?

I'm done. Now bring me a towel.

GALLAGHER IS AN UNFUNNY, PATHETIC, DRIED-UP PIECE OF DOG CRAP

N MY LAST COLUMN, I made a passing reference to the "comedian" Gallagher, a reference that took half a sentence, roughly the same amount of good material that Gallagher has produced since 1983.

I hate to waste any more ink on this dried up monkey turd with male pattern baldness, especially since I could be using this space to discuss things of far greater importance, like, say, anal warts or uncontrolled bowel discharge.

And yet it must be done. A friend of mine got screwed over by Gallagher; and it is up to me to relate this story, because my friend does not work for a renowned, widely distributed alternative newspaper. And neither do I, but at least I have a platform other than a unread blog.

Recently one of my comedian buddies was scheduled to be the opening act for Gallagher in Becker, MN, a town made famous when it was portrayed on television by Ted Danson. Anyway, my friend—whom we shall refer to as "Funny Guy"—was on stage only minutes before he was interrupted by Gallagher—whom we shall refer to as "Pathetic Dried-Up Dicklicker."

It seems that Pathetic Dried-Up Dicklicker didn't like Funny Guy's first two jokes and began criticizing Funny Guy's act in front of the audience, who perhaps believed this to be part of Gallagher's act—which it probably was; because let's face it, he hasn't had anything approaching an original act since he somehow convinced an agent that he had talent.

Of course, Gallagher had apparently planned in advance to interrupt Funny Guy's act, as it had become part of Gallagher's schtick to do so; consequently, he was better prepared with insults than my unsuspecting friend. What followed was several minutes of public humiliation of Funny Guy by this Pathetic Dried-Up Dicklicker, which is a little like getting your ass handed to you in a bar fight by Gary Coleman.

Finally, Gallagher allowed Funny Guy to continue his act…for about two more minutes, after which he came back on stage, told Funny Guy that he wasn't funny (presumably because Funny Guy's act consisted of actually telling jokes instead of smashing produce items), and booted him off the stage. Funny Guy had spent five hours on the road to do less than three minutes of material and get humiliated by a guy who makes Carrot Top look like Mark Twain.

Unfortunately, I must briefly play the straight guy here: It's bad enough when a performer interrupts another performer's act. It's particularly sleazy when the established act dumps on an unknowner. It's bullying in the barest form. Just because Gallagher had his head repeatedly shoved in the toilet during his formative years for being an effeminate, narcissistic, pharmaceutical trainwreck doesn't mean he has to take it out on those with more talent.

More to the point, should anyone—anyone at ALL, even John Kerry—be taking comedy advice from Gallagher? The funniest thing to come from Gallagher in the past few decades was when his brother, Gallagher II, let his sledgehammer slip out of his greasy paws and slammed an audience member in the head.

(Incidentally, yes, despite initial news reports, it was Gallagher II, not Gallagher, to whom this incident occurred, although one could argue that it was the best thing to happen in either of their careers. It was certainly a mercy blow for the audience member.)

Folks may recall that Gallagher sued Gallagher II, saying that his name brought "confusion to the marketplace." And I agree. It's confusing how either of them find work.

More confusing is why anyone would want to be "II" to Gallagher. I mean, "George Carlin 2" I could understand. But consider that "II"'s tend to be worse than the original (i.e., *Jaws 2* is not as good as *Jaws*; and *Jaws 3-D* was so bad it made audiences blow chunks that seemed to fly right at you, mainly because they were coming from the guy in the next seat).

In any event, if the level of suckiness is determined by the number following the act, then the original Gallagher should actually be known as "Gallagher XXXVII." And Gallagher II should be known as "Gallagher With the Infinity Sign Behind It."

But we can still get a few yuks out of Gallagher yet. Here's how: Get yourself a sledgehammer. Then pick up a VHS copy (used) of *Gallagher: Maddest*. "More like 'Flattest'!" you shout, and BAM!

"What's this?" you ask. "A copy of Gallagher's *Stuck in the 60's* [sic]? Now it's going to be *Struck Into Pieces*!" BAM! "What? *Best of Gallagher Vol. 2*?! What is it, two hours of Gallagher walking off stage?" BAM! "This one's called *Over Your Head*. Let's see if it goes over the moon!" BAM! "*Overboard*? Meet 'Under Mallet'!" BAM! "*We Need a Hero*? You're about to need a plastic surgeon!" BAM!

Much like Gallagher's career…I'm done.

THE TITLE TO THIS COLUMN HAS BEEN CENSORED BY THE FCC

THERE'S BEEN A LOT OF talk about how Barack Hussein Obama became president despite a distinctly non-European-sounding name. After all, the name Hussein is shared with a dictator; Obama is one letter short of Osama; and Barack translates from Swahili as "terrorists' pal who is also a lousy bowler."

Of course, we would find a lot of funny names if we looked at our vice-presidents, like Schuyler Colfax, William Rufus de Vane King, Spiro Agnew, or George Bush. And pity the poor history teacher who had to maintain order in the classroom while talking about Andrew Johnson's vice-president, Poopy Cockenballs.

Ha, ha! I'm just joking in that last paragraph, of course. Can you imagine a vice-president named Spiro Agnew? That's just silly.

This leads me to St. Louis County Auditor Donald Dicklich. Now, I'm not going to make fun of Mr. Dicklich just because his name happens to correspond with an act that is illegal for me to purchase. I'm sure he is, as John

McCain might say, not an Arab but instead an honorable family man.

But what amazes me is that Dicklich is an elected official. Voters actually had to pull the lever for Dicklich. And they apparently did so, despite the fact that his office stationery is the only kind in county government to come with a parental advisory.

Personally, I find it inspiring to see someone overcome such an obvious hurdle to become a successful public official. Or perhaps voters were simply rejecting the extreme positions of his challenger, Harry Beaver.

But the brutal world of politics is nothing compared to the ultimate bloody battlefield that is called "grade school playground." I'm sure that this discussion was often repeated in the House of Dicklich:

Donny: Dad, the kids at school beat me up again! Can't we change our name?

Dicklich Sr.: No, son. We're proud to be Dicklichs. Your grandfather was a Dicklich, and his grandfather before him. We are a hard, sturdy people, and we must remain firm. Now go throw rocks at the Putz children next door.

Now, I'm told he pronounces his name "Dick-litch," but I don't believe it. It's obviously a German name, and Germany is where we get a lot of words that sound inherently dirty, including, but not limited to: dich, fahrt, sechs, ausholen and dichkunst. And I believe this is intentional. In fact, Nazis deliberately spoke German to American soldiers during WWII to make them start giggling uncontrollably.

Seriously, these people need to wash out their mouths with soap. Especially when one considers the things that Germans put in their mouths, like bratwurst, sauerkraut, and the occasional dicklich.

Perhaps worse than Dicklich is a tombstone I found

during one my nightly stalkings through the cemetery. The name on it was "Schmuck." I believe this had to be his real name, and not the workings of a less-than-bereaved widow.

I mean, going through the effort of making and installing an insulting tombstone is generally more trouble than most people would go through to get back at a deceased former boss. Most would be content to merely dance on the grave or whizz on the flowers. (The more industrious ex-employee might dig up the corpse and rape it, but any boss who pissed off a former employee with that kind of dedication most likely deserves an unpleasant rest.)

So it's safe to say that the guy's name really was Schmuck. To say that this raises a few questions is an understatement. Perhaps the most pressing is, Was it a suicide? And if so, how did he botch it? There wasn't an epitaph, but I'm guessing it would've read, "I didn't think the gun was loaded," or "I should have packed a parachute," or "Don't get between Sarah Palin and a moose."

But am I in a position to make fun of people's names? Absolutely. I may have the name of a cartoon character, but I'm not a Dicklich or a Schmuck. At least, I'm not the capital-letter versions of those. My name translates easily into modern English as "son of John, son of Ja." "Ja," of course, is German for "yes," as in, "Yes, this guy sure plays with his johnson."

Incidentally, I'm not sure who coined the word "johnson" as slang for the jimmy. Presumably, it was the same person who used the word "bush" for the female yoo-hoo. That means, of course, that we've had several presidents with names more offensive than Barack Hussein Obama.

I think we should agree that the new slang for "asshole" should be "cheney."

I'm done.

OBAMA WILL WALK BOW-LEGGED, AND OTHER 2009 PREDICTIONS

ONE MEMORABLE CHILDHOOD XMASTIME, I was taken to church to view a film, which concluded with the main character getting lost in a blizzard and dying. Watching the climactic scene, I intuitively deduced the film's message: God helps those who help themselves, unless "themselves" get severe hypothermia.

But the film's denouement assured us that everything was hunky-dorey, because the dead man had been a man of faith and therefore went to Heaven, where he was surrounded by toys, never had to do homework, and everything tasted like peppermint, including one's own poo.

The message became a little clearer: Die, and your Christian friends will be happy for you. Needless to say, this had a negative impact on my Sunday School attendance.

I'm sure there was some mention in the film about God's Plan, which is every Christian's last line of defense. There's considerably less talk about what happens when God's Plan conflicts with *My* Plan, which involves, among other things, not dying in a fucking blizzard.

So yet again I chose to forgo Xmas this year and celebrate instead Dec. 28th, the birthday of Spider-Man co-creator Stan Lee, despite what I call the "War on Stan Lee's Birthday," which culminates in store clerks' insistence on saying the politically correct "Merry Xmas" instead of the more appropriate, "With great power comes great responsibility."

One holiday that remains largely uncontroversial is New Year's Day, although there is some dispute as to whether "But it happened *last year*!" is a valid excuse for having felt up a co-worker at a New Year's party the night before.

But the best thing about a new year, other than getting to hang one's *Sexy Asian Kitty Firefighters* calendar, is new year predictions.

As everyone knows, the winter solstice naturally increases one's ability for prognostication, so consider these forecasts to be merely history that has not happened yet:

*George W. Bush, despite admonitions from the publishing world, will begin his autobiography, which will have greater factual inaccuracies than a typical Superman comicbook and be rejected by hundreds of publishers for its overuse of the word "varmints." Eventually it will be published under the title *Don't Blame Me, I Voted for Kerry*! after learning that the title *Mein Kampf* has already been taken.

*Karl Rove is also penning a memoir, in which he claims he will "name names," and list all those who refused to recognize George W. Bush as a legitimately elected president. The book will be entitled *The Phone Book*.

*Obama will set aside political considerations and instead focus on upholding U.S. and international law by punishing former Bush administration officials who besmirched the

Constitution with massive abuses of power, including torture, warrantless wiretaps, and an illegal invasion.

Ha ha ha! No, seriously, Obama's term will be begin with impeachment hearings, following his arrest for carrying a Glock in the groin of his sweatpants.

*Rachel Ray will snap and stick a steak knife into Regis Philbin's forehead. Millions of shocked viewers will watch the clip on YouTube and ask, "How come Kelly Ripa never showed that kind of initiative?"

*There will be seventeen Paul Rudd comedies in 2009. Two of them will be funny.

*You will not win the lottery. It will be won by some dumb hick who says it "won't change him," even though he'll become a total dick overnight. He claims he'll spend it on his kids—which is true, if by "kids," he means "gambling debts."

*Heather Mills will adopt a minefield. The minefield will sue for dissolution, claiming emotional abuse.

*Apple will begin marketing a sexual stimulator that fits in the front pants pocket. It will be called the iPud.

*Sarah Palin will compete with her daughter's new in-laws to see who will be the biggest family embarrassment. It will not be pretty, but you will still have to look.

*The news media will constantly scare the hell out of you over things you can't do anything about, like global warming, nukes in the Middle East, the economic crisis, and Tom Cruise.

*God will forsake you. The turning point will be your sixth act of check-kiting.

*Following his impeachment, ex-Gov. Rod Blagojevich will get a job on QVC, where he will shamelessly hawk random consonants. They will be overpriced, underperform, and smell like mousse.

*A Jessica Simpson song will be grossly overplayed. It

will be Exhibit A when she goes to trial to face charges of instigating mass suicide.

*Shark Week on the Discovery channel will return after a few short messages.

*Six words: Director of Homeland Security Bill Ayers.

*Ford, GM and Chrysler will finally turn a profit after they stop calling their products "cars" and instead call them "redneck lawn ornaments."

*A sports star will be involved in a drug scandal, there will be a spat on *The View*, and Lindsay Lohan will do more blow.

Happy 2009. I'm done.

RAPE ISN'T ALWAYS FUNNY ...AND OTHER REASONS WHY I WASN'T INVITED TO THE INAUGURATION

BY THE TIME YOU READ this, Barack Obama will be sworn in as president and will have surrendered to the terrorists. It is a harsh world you are awaking to, one where our new terrorist leaders torture, spy on their citizens, and are totally surprised at their own attacks, which they will blame on Bill Clinton.

Obama has apparently decided not to prosecute crimes committed under the Bush era, saying that he wants to look forward rather than backward. And I agree: I, for one, am looking forward to seeing Bush and Cheney on trial in The Hague.

A lot has been made about the history-making of America's first black president. Technically, he's only half-black, which means he can play basketball but has the dancing rhythm of a three-legged cat with vertigo.

Interestingly, there's little discussion about the fact that we once had an Indian vice-president. Charles Curtis, VP under Herbert Hoover, was not only half-Indian, but he even bragged about it, taking pictures with his Kaw headdress, displaying Indian artifacts in his office, and occasionally dying of small pox.

Curtis's brazen embrace of his lineage is particularly significant when one considers how Obama, during the campaign season, did everything to assure white America that he was one of them. He kept his car stereo turned down, tipped big in restaurants, and didn't shout at the movie screen, a tactic that worked until he tried to hail a taxi and revealed that he was invisible to cab drivers.

But in 1929, we had a half-Indian vice-president a heartbeat away from the presidency, and *nobody cared*. There was no talk about whether America was ready for an Indian president. No talk about whether Curtis was "Indian enough" to win the Indian vote. And there were no crazy, spit-take-inducing conspiracy theories on *Hannity and Colmes*:

Hannity: I'm telling you, Curtis is a secret Earth spiritualist! If he becomes president, he won't swear on the Bible! He'll just swear in on his oral tradition of ancestral legends!

Colmes: You realize you're not making any sense, right?

Hannity: Why would I start now?

Another curiosity about the inauguration: If he's not impeached soon, embattled Governor and hair model Rod Blagojevich will be attending. Yes, B-Rod got tickets to the event because he is, on paper, still the acting governor, much like Bush is still technically president, and Joe the Plumber is technically a celebrity.

Unfortunately, both not-senator-yet Al Franken and not-senator-anymore Norm Coleman are also planning to attend the inauguration. And the National Mall was not built to hold Coleman's pompadour, Franken's Jew-fro, and B-Rod's mullet-slash-dead raccoon hat. As in real life, the best hair at the party will be the black guy's.

In any case, the disputed 2008 senate race between Franken and Coleman will still be in full swing, hence the dual invitations and not having one of the non-senators watching the inauguration with his unemployed ass parked on his living-room couch.

Remember when Coleman said that Franken should spare Minnesotans a long, costly battle over the election and simply concede? Ah, but that was ten weeks ago. Lots of things have changed since then, except Coleman's knack for flaming hypocrisy.

But now it's time for Franken to get on with the business of humiliating our state. And I know he will, because I was led to believe so after recently participating in a telephone poll in which the caller asked what could be charitably called leading questions:

She asked, "Would you vote for a senatorial candidate whose only previous experience was being a comedian who joked about rape?"

"Would I!" I said. "I wish that guy were running! Lady, I *am* a comedian, and I've joked about raping *Christ*." This is, in fact, 100% true. I won't repeat that joke here, because, as my editor informs me, sponsors apparently frown on associating themselves with Christ-humpers.

I don't know why, but most polls I've been a participant in have had a right-wing slant. For instance, I was once asked by a pollster if I supported a minimum wage hike. When I said yes, she asked, "Would you still support it if it could be proven that the raise would hurt small businesses and would go mostly only to teenagers?"

"If you could prove that, then no, I wouldn't support it,"

I told her. "And if I were a lesbian, I'd be banging Rachel Maddow."

Another thing these polls have in common—and I've confirmed this with other poll takers—is that there's always one oddball, off-the-subject question that comes out of right field. They ask questions like, "Are you a Minnesota resident?" Yes. "Did you vote in the last election?" Yes. "Are you registered to vote?" Yes. "Do you like to have sex with dead animals?"

"Hey!" I said. "I just said I'm from Minnesota, not Wisconsin!"

And now that I've offended blacks, Indians, lesbians and Cheeseheads,…at last, I'm done.

YOU CAN STOP LYING ABOUT
THE SUPER BOWL NOW

VERY YEAR, FOOTBALL FANS GET excited about the Super Bowl, only to tell me later, "It sucked!" Apparently the Super Bowl is one of those ideas that is better in theory than in practice, much like the decision to marry Amy Winehouse.

The buzz around this year's Bowl has been generally positive, but you're not fooling anyone. It sucked this year, too, and it will always suck, and here's why: Because it's goddamn *football*.

Football and golf are two sports that, when they come on television, actually make me think things like, "Gee, I wonder what's on the Weather Channel?" or "Hey, maybe this Ben Affleck film isn't so bad after all." Or even, "Say, what's showing on the Dog-Shit-Rotting-On-a-Hot-Day Channel? Chihuahua shit in a Mexican parking lot? *¡Que interestante!*

Seriously, I'd rather watch four hours of static. At least then I could be alone with my thoughts, and all the inane and occasionally racist commentary would be coming only from me.

Sure, those of you who watched the game in Tucson were, due to a feed mixup, inadvertently treated to ten seconds of hardcore porn, including full-frontal male nudity and what had to be the best…touchdown dance…*ever*. But for the rest of the country, if you wanted to see a huge dick during the Super Bowl, you had to settle for Matt Lauer.

So don't tell me you loved the Super Bowl when all you can remember is the ads. This kind of historical revisionism belongs strictly to Bush's legacy tour.

Speaking of which, in his final address to the nation, Bush said, "You may not agree with some of the tough decisions I have made, but I hope you can agree that I was willing to make the tough decisions."

Here's the thing, George: *They were the wrong decisions.* You don't get points for that. Try it on your next multiple choice test:

You: "Well, teacher, you may not agree that kangaroos come from Austria, but we can agree that filled in the dot!"

Teacher: "Actually, you didn't. You just wrote 'Lizard People' all over your test."

You: "But at least I spelled it right!"

Teacher: "You spelled 'Peeple' with two 'e's! Why don't you go back to eating your paste? You already got half the jar down."

In any case, it seems that making decisions is the barest minimum we would expect of a president. Apparently, Bush's job could have been done just as well by a monkey with a magic 8-ball.

"Should I invade Iraq?" [Shakes ball.] *Yes.*

"Should I fix the economy?" [Shakes.] *Try again later.*

"Am I the greatest president ever?" [Shakes.] *It will take historians at least a generation to properly assess your administration, and when they do, they will find that all your*

misfortunes were the fault of Bill Clinton. In the meantime,
continue to throw feces at Nancy Pelosi.

As far as the real decider during the previous dynasty
is concerned, it's fitting that the parting image we have of
Dick Cheney is of him sitting in a wheelchair, dressed in
a black hat and trenchcoat as if he were Blofeld from the
James Bond films. (Coincidentally, Blofeld recruits most of
his henchmen from Halliburton.)

In fact, comedian Jon Stewart noted that all Cheney
was missing was the cat on his lap. That, of course, is totally
unfair. Cheney long ago had the cat waterboarded. In
fairness to Cheney, the cat was Persian.

Some more cheap parting shots to those who are leaving
us:

*Norm Coleman: Your legal team recently cited *Bush
V. Gore* in their ongoing lawsuit to overturn Al Franken's
senate election. Apparently, they didn't read the clause in
the 2000 decision in which the Supreme Court specifically
stated that the case should not be used as precedent, because
it was an "extraordinary circumstance," which is another
way of saying, "Even we realize that this decision has all the
legal merit of a typical episode of *Ally McBeal*."

*Rod Blagojevich: Don't feel bad that, after having your
ass kissed by D.L. Hughley, you had it handed to you by
David Letterman. There will always be a place on TV for
narcissistic sociopaths, as Glenn Beck can testify.

*Tom Daschle: Sure, it may seem unfair that Timothy
Geithner was too important to pass over for a cabinet
position because of tax evasion, while you were tossed like
Kate Bosworth's cookies. But now you can go back to the
same thing you were doing when you were Democratic
minority leader: getting mistaken for a doormat.

*Joe the Plumber: Please, just go. Just…just go. And take some of Blago's hair with you.

I'm done.

HERE'S ANOTHER DAMN COLUMN THAT WILL EMBARRASS MY FAMILY

READ THAT THE OCTUPLET MOTHER had a makeover to make herself look like Angelina Jolie. I confess to feeling a certain amount of vindication about this, because it proves what I've been trying to tell people for years: Angelina Jolie is *ugly*.

Worse yet, the woman has been offered to star in a porn video. I'm guessing it will be called, I don't know, *Birth of a Nation? Slumdog Whitetrash? Stretch Marks the Spot? 101 Fetuses?* (I saw one publication suggest *Octopussy*, but I'm too classy to repeat that here.)

Apparently, her co-star had already been cast but had to be replaced after he fell and disappeared into that endless cavern she calls a uterus.

Seriously, it's bad enough she's reproducing; we should not have to see her naked. It's no wonder the woman had to go "in vitro," because, speaking as a typical horny heterosexual male, I wouldn't stick it in her if I thought I'd strike oil. And you're reading this from a guy who once humped his couch.

Oh, relax, I'm just kidding! I've actually humped the couch several times.

But maybe Angelina Jolie looks good in one's peripheral vision. This has probably happened to other guys from time to time: You see a woman out of the corner of your eye and find her attractive, because she's roughly the right body type, has nice-enough hair, and is presumably alive.

And then you look directly at the woman. Your eyes begin to water and see spots, and you upchuck some of the chili you had last Thursday. Because it's then you realize that, for a brief instant, you were momentarily attracted to Julia Roberts.

I realize we're pre-programmed to keep an eye out for potential mates. But being attracted to Julia Roberts, however briefly, can be counter-productive to the reproductive cycle. It can trigger nausea and an aversion to sex, which, coincidentally, is a similar result one gets from viewing Julia Roberts' filmography.

However, you can recover. Unfortunately, it won't be until the second President Palin term. And by then, you'll be too busy recovering from a guilty pleasure that I call the "erection of shame."

It's a similar feeling guys get when we sort of, kind of, more-or-less accidentally self-pleasure ourselves to an ugly chick.

I don't know what causes this phenomenon. Sometimes a woman with severe appearance deficits just kind of pops into your head while you're enjoying the Sports Illustrated swimsuit issue, and then, well, she kind of pops out again.

It's unclear how we men are supposed to feel about this. On one hand (probably the dominant hand), you want to celebrate a job well done. On the other hand (the subservient hand?), you realize that you accomplished an orgasm by first fantasizing about Marisa Miller, and then fantasizing about an old classmate in college, the one who has a mouth that looks like a whale's vagina.

What's the proper etiquette in this situation? Do you have to call her in the morning?

Guy: "Say, Debbie, about last night: I didn't mean to just towel myself and run, but I really did have to get to work."

Ugly chick: "Who the hell is this?"

Guy: "It's Jason? I yanked it on you last night? Look, here's the thing: I'm kind of already yanking it on another woman. It's no one you know—OK, it's Jessica Alba, but never mind that.

"Look, it's not you, it's me: *I* think you're hideous. And that's totally my fault. This just isn't a good time in my life to indulge in a whale-vagina fetish… I'm speaking to a dial tone now, aren't I?"

The important thing, I suppose, is to focus on the positive. In this case, the make-up sex with your pinup of Marisa Miller.

There's an upside to the Octomom story, too. As soon as all her kids become teenagers, she'll jump in front of a train.

I'm done.

I'M THE REASON YOUR UMD DEGREE IS WORTHLESS

PPARENTLY WHAT FEW READERS I have tend to be college students, which I guess makes sense. College students have that rare combination of being (a) old enough to be literate, and (b) young enough to still laugh at poop jokes.

The irony doesn't escape me. Because if you're a student at the U of MN-Duluth, I'm at least partially responsible for the fact that your parents wasted tons of money getting you a degree that will be valuable only if you use it to wipe your underemployed ass.

Granted, I majored in English, which means my master's degree was essentially a resume for Burger King. It's like telling people you got your law degree from Pat Robertson U.

As an institution, UMD is my mortal enemy, right up there with al-Qaeda, the Bush II administration, and fat guys in Speedos. UMD is responsible for my worst educational Hell, and this is coming from a guy who barely survived junior-high phy ed class, where "dodgeball" could better be described as "smash-the-four-eyed-sissy's-face-in"-ball.

For the sake of brevity, I'll limit myself to only two

anecdotes to prove that UMD is run by evil pinheads who are so incompetent, they were given bonuses by AIG:

(1) UMD lost two sets of my transcripts *and* my health records. This is bad enough, but my real beef is that, each time this occurred, a UMD pinhead would act like this *never happened before*, despite the fact that not only had it happened to me multiple times, but I knew numerous other students that it also happened to. The attitude of the staff was always the same: "If we can't find them, they don't exist." Presumably, if any of *them* went missing, then perhaps *they* wouldn't exist, a prospect that was looking more and more appetizing by the day.

In fact, in one instance, one pinhead told me that *I* was to blame for the missing transcripts. After all, I was such a doofus to send my transcripts to the *admissions* office instead of the *transcripts* office. Yes, that was stupid of me, taking the word of the UMD handbook, which said—and I quote, with the taste of vomit in my mouth—"Please send a copy of your transcripts to the *admissions* office." [Sarcastic emphasis added.]

And by the way, UMD: seriously? You can't get someone to sort through what must be tons of missent mail to walk down the hallway and take it to the proper office? May I suggest, I don't know, a *college student*? For Christ's sake, they work for Pepsi and a bag of Fritos. It's the closest thing to slave labor we legally allow in this country.

(2) I had to have a college professor sign a slip to join his lit class. When I brought the slip to the clerk, she tore it up and threw it away. "He didn't check the

box in the corner," she explained. "So we have no way of knowing if you forged his signature."

I mean, you have got to be fucking kidding me.

Even a UMD graduate can figure this one out: If I could forge his signature, why couldn't I forge a fucking check in a box?! Needless to say, I took another permission slip, forged the prof's signature, checked the box, and voila: Before I knew it, I was being bored by lectures from a professor who was as good at checking boxes as he was at shutting the hell up.

But I got my revenge on UMD when I single-handedly lowered the campus's academic standards. It was a plan so ingenious, so clever, so conniving, that I couldn't even have planned or conceived it. So I didn't. Like every thing else in life, it was a happy accident. Here's how my sinister plan was executed:

I failed my master's exam on the first try. This is nothing to ashamed about; and besides, like everything that happened in the 1990s, it was all Bill Clinton's fault.

But now I need to set the stage for my second try: Unlike my first attempt, when I dressed in a button-down shirt and black dress pants, I arrived at my exam—dirty, unshaven, and unwashed, like a slightly less masculine Paris Hilton—directly from my job at the U.S. Postal Service. Keep in mind that this was the mid-90s, in which postal shootings were more common than Rush Limbaugh divorces.

[Note: In fact, it was around this time that the phrase "going postal" gained currency. As this phrase is grossly unfair to the scores of postal employees who have never killed anyone, we now more tastefully refer to this phenomenon as "going high school."]

In any event, I proceeded to fail the exam even worse than before. In fact, during the oral exam, my answers were so bad, I heard more outright laughter from my professors than I heard at my first collegiate sexual experience.

And yet, the professors passed me. This, despite the chairman actually telling me point blank that he thought that I had done insufficient work in his class, and that I had not properly studied for the test; and furthermore, the hooker at my first collegiate sexual experience thought I had a tiny penis.

So why, then, did my professors give me a degree? They either (a) really, really, liked me; or (b) in light of the postal violence in the news, they were afraid that I'd kill them. I prefer to think it's (a), which goes a long way in explaining why I twice failed that stupid exam.

Ironically, I didn't really care if they failed me. I had a job at the postal service that I knew I would never leave, and that my English degree, like every other English degree, would be worthless.

Well, almost worthless. It did a good job cleaning my ass before I flushed it.

I'm done.

I LIKE IT WHEN HUNTERS SHOOT EACH OTHER

ALTHOUGH I KNOW THE NAMES "Columbine" and "Virginia Tech," I'm pleased to report that I cannot remember the names of the pricks behind those tragedies. I have similar pride in my inability to name a single Eminem track, more than one American Idol winner, or many of my numerous high-school traumas involving pot and public nudity.

It's clear from the news recently that there's a flaw in this whole "blaze of infamy" you mass-murderers are apparently seeking. There's been way too many of you jackasses lately, and your name will be forgotten as soon as the next news cycle, or until the next Madonna adoption, whichever comes first.

You obviously haven't really considered the advantage to just plugging yourself. People will remember your name for just as long, except they won't think of you as a total asshole. They'll think, "Gee, we sure wish we treated Batshit McCrazy better when he was alive!"

See? You get exactly you want: Pity and guilt from people who spurned you. Plus, your death means that you'll provide work for clean-up crews, *and* the government won't have to pay your Social Security. In this economy, you'll be a downright *hero*. Everyone wins.

At least one of the pricks involved in the recent string of shootings was apparently a gun nut who worried that Obama was going to pass tougher gun laws. Of course, this idiot is probably going to *inspire* tougher laws, which shows that gun nuts have no sense of irony to go along with their no sense of reason.

(As an internationally beloved cartoonist once said, "Why is it that gun nuts are the last people in the world who should have guns?")

At the risk of perpetuating the fears of you Second Amendment distorters, you need to hear something: You've proven that you can't play nice with your toys, so we're taking them away.

"But Mr. Johnson," you ask, "what about hunters?"

First of all, thank you for the respectful tone. That goes a long way with me. But here's my answer to your question: Fuck hunters.

Look, I've known some very nice people who are hunters, but the cold truth is that I love it when they shoot each other. In fact, I have a scale of hilarity involved in hunting accidents, based on the severity or lethality of the shot, and how closely related the victim is to the shooter.

Dick Cheney non-fatally shoots a lawyer in the face? Amusing.

A hunter shoots his own brother in the leg, forever crippling him? Funny.

A 14-year-old kid splatters his dad's brains against the side of a dutch elm? Side-splitting, eye-watering, nose-running, holy-crap-I-wet-myself fucking *hilarious*.

Granted, this may be an extreme position. However, hunters have no reason to hunt other than bloodlust, despite their argument that hunting is no different from killing animals to eat meat, or clubbing to death Carson Daly.

Yes, I do eat meat. But here's the difference between eating hamburgers and hunting: I don't get a boner from shooting a cow in the face. Just because I like eating an animal doesn't mean I get my rocks off killing it and watching it die, okay?

So you hunters kill because you enjoy it. Fine. I can respect that to a certain extent. But given that adult bucks are about as intelligent as the average first-grader, your target is only about six IQ points short of making you a playground sniper.

"But Mr. Johnson," you say, "hunters thin the herd so deer don't starve."

First of all, I'm glad you're keeping that respectful tone even after I laughed about splattering your brains. But you're still full of shit.

Never mind that you've just employed the South Park "we-have-to-kill-them-or-they'll-die" argument. Never mind that the most overpopulated species on this planet is man, thanks partly to Octomom and to states (other than Texas) that refuse to execute the mentally challenged, which has more than once saved the life of Karl Rove.

No, here's where your argument drops dead: You don't just shoot the starving ones. In fact, the healthier the kill, the prouder you are. I will apologize to any hunter who can honestly tell me that he shoots only those deer that are suffering from wasting disease and look like Mary-Kate Olsen after a fresh protein purge.

Also, one may notice a slight power imbalance in the fact that hunters have guns and deer are, by and large, rather lacking in cop-killer firepower.

I knew one hunter who claimed that there was "no unfair advantage" in the fact that he had a gun and the deer did not, because "the deer is in its natural element."As if the deer would be off-limits if he saw it in a Wal-Mart parking lot.

By the way, isn't this your house? Goodie. You're in your natural element.

Now I'm going to place your head on the wall of my study, use your skin as a carpet, and tell people I picked you off at 25 yards, even though you just happened to stupidly wander in front of my gun looking for oats.

I'm done.

POLITICAL MODERATES CAN SUCK IT

'M NOT SURE WHAT IT says about the modern Republican party that Arlen Specter is considered a "moderate," except that it's a little like saying Michele Bachmann is just moderately crazy because she doesn't publicly display her urine in jars.

Sure, Specter has a pathetic 81% rating from the Christian Coalition, a lofty 27% rating from the League of Conservation Voters, and a mere 67% Republican voting record, all of which make Republicans so angry they could throw him in the Potomac after wrapping a boulder in his jowls.

The media like to lump Specter in with other political moderates like Joe Lieberman, Ben Nelson, Evan Bayh, George Voinovich, and John McCain. What do these figures have in common to get the "moderate" label?

Oh, yeah. They're all douchebags.

Annoyingly, moderates cling to an air of superiority—or at least, it's an air of something. They also suffer from a persecution complex, believing that both major parties hate them because of their principles and not because of the real reason, i.e., their overbearing douchebaggery.

Of course, moderates serve an important function.

After all, someone has to have the political wisdom to vote against food stamps, veterans' benefits, and children's health care coverage, yet retain the compassion necessary to resist drowning kittens on the Sabbath.

The truth is that moderates are the same people who gave Bush an 83% approval rating at the beginning of the Iraq War and now oppose it with no sense of complicity. And they gave Bush two terms despite liberals' Cassandra-like warning that allowing an illiterate potato-head with a fetish for killing people just might be a bad idea.

I've come to the conclusion that "moderate" is applied to any politician who is wrong a mere 50% of the time or more. Moderates are, in essence, what political scientists call "the Duh group."

Incidentally, one will notice that even Republicans now admit that Bush was an historical mistake. In fact, to hear them explain it, they *always* hated Bush! That Bush guy makes them sick! Ptui!

So if Republicans hated this guy, and Democrats hated this guy, how the hell did he get to president for eight goddamn years? Apparently, Bush was just some carny charlatan, who used his magic verbal skills to talk them into putting all their money in Bear Stearns, or using a slang for testicle sucking as their political protest theme.

Another good example is gay rights, which has come a long way since 1993, when the media obsessed over the idea that Bill Clinton was actually going to let (gasp!) *gays* serve in the military! Is he crazy? Why, soldiers shower together, and a gay soldier might see a straight soldier's ding-dong!

That obsession lasted for a few more years until the media obsessed about something more pertinent, like the fact that a straight woman saw Bill Clinton's ding-dong.

Now, I realize that you younger readers are confused by this. After all, you weren't paying attention to politics in the '90s, as you were more properly focused on watching Melissa Joan Hart develop breasts on *Sabrina the Teenage Witch*.

So you're probably thinking, "But gay rights is *still* a big issue!" But no, it's not. The anti-gay-marriage debate was so heated in the '90s, it pressured a Democratic president to sign the Defense of Marriage Act, an act whose name immediately conjured up visions of gay people storming into married couples' homes and forcing them to sign divorce papers while dancing to Ricky Martin.

Now, California's anti-gay marriage Prop 8 amendment victory notwithstanding, the trend in this country is toward gay marriage, as evidenced by the fact that even *Iowa* now has gay couples, a fact that should embarrass Minnesota into adopting the practice, or at least hiring Bruce Vilanch to redecorate the state.

There is also greater reception to that heretofore heretical idea of gays in the military, which had previously been blocked by "moderates" like Sam Nunn and Colin Powell. Unfortunately, this is mainly because Bush's extended military tours have caused recruiters to lower their standards to include psychotics, the mentally retarded, and other former members of Bush's Justice Department.

But who changed in the gay rights debate? I still have the same radical, far-left positions I had fifteen years ago. Moderates are only now taking the same position, proving we lefties were *right all along*. Not that I'm unhappy you've changed your minds, but where were you moderates back in 1993?

Oh, right. You were being douchebags. So excuse me if I don't take your health care proposals too seriously. Especially with that huge boulder in your jowls.

I'm done.

PICKING ON OLD PEOPLE, ASIAN KIDS, AND OTHER GROUPS I CAN TAKE IN A FIGHT

JOHN MCCAIN RECENTLY ASKED PRESIDENT Obama for a posthumous pardon for Jack Johnson, a black man who in 1913 was convicted of the "crime" of having sex with a white woman. McCain held a press conference announcing, "Now is the time to pardon Jack Johnson."

Really, senator? *Now* is the time? Wouldn't a better time have been…I dunno…1913?! "Now" is actually the 96th year of unfortunate procrastination.

Don't get me wrong, senator: I applaud the sentiment. But you do realize that you didn't have to wait until there was a black guy in the White House, right? Take Bill Clinton, for example: There was a guy who understood being persecuted for having sex with a white woman.

But perhaps we can forgive McCain of having left the issue on the back burner all these years. It happened in 1913, after all, while he was busy having a youthful indiscretion with Helen Taft.

You know what? That's a cheap shot. We all know that

with age comes wisdom, even if that wisdom consists of putting on your national ticket a moose-eating hick who thinks men co-existed with the dinosaurs and propelled their cars with by sticking their feet through the floorboards.

Incidentally, when John McCain drove his prehistoric, feet-propelled car…he drove it with his blinker on. Fifteen miles under the speed limit. In the passing lane.

Okay, those are also cheap shots. It's just a stereotype that old people can't drive. And like all stereotypes, they're unfair, overly broad, and 100% true.

In fact, it seems that the only time we hear of old people stepping on the gas pedal is when they're plowing through shoppers at a sidewalk flea market.

But I'm above making jokes about old people's driving. I'm a *thinking* comedian, and I'm therefore plagued by the question as to *why* they drive so slow. If anyone should be in a hurry, shouldn't it be old folks?

"I gotta find a restroom before I overfill this adult diaper!"

"I gotta get home so I can crawl into a nice, cozy death bed!"

"Slam on the gas, Mabel! It's 4:30, and the coffin store closes at five!"

And in case you're wondering, yes, at a certain age, the funeral parlor becomes "the coffin store." Just ask your grandparents.

And why aren't there more elderly serial killers? They could kill just about anyone who takes the last loaf of day-old bread, and what are the cops going to do? Put them away for *life*? Goodness, they might get twenty to thirty…days.

But before I get criticized for using stereotypes, I'll point out that not all stereotypes are negative. For example, as several recent university studies show, Asian kids are better at math.

That's right: They conducted studies to learn what anyone who attended public schools could tell you. Presumably, they got their funding from the National Educational Council of Freakin' *Duh*.

There's a reason this stereotype exists: It's true. This is why I struggled with my algebra exams until blood ran from my ear, while the Chan kid had already completed it, turned his paper over, and designed a perfectly functioning hybrid vehicle.

Not the plans for a vehicle, mind you. The actual vehicle.

A long-standing myth is that Asian kids did better math simply because they didn't want to shame their families. In Japan, if you fail math, you are expected to redeem the family name by throwing yourself in front of a subway, preferably one that leaves Point A at 78 kph and meets you at Point B, traveling at 0 kph.

This, of course, is in stark contrast to families in America, where you can dance naked on a reality TV show with your underwear on your face and have your mother shout at the neighbors: "*I taught him how to do that!*"

But the "family-shame" myth is debunked by a study from the U of Saskatchewan, which found that Asian kids did better at math regardless of upbringing; i.e., even when they're raised by us typically lazy North American parents, who get their jobs by cheating off an Asian guy's resume.

One inter-university study between American and Chinese educators tried to make the case that the problem lay with the teachers, and perhaps they have a point. I never understood why we had to learn when two trains would meet at a certain point after traveling at a certain speed. The answer is always the same: "Who gives a crap, because one of trains is always twenty minutes late, and the other train's engineer derailed while texting his girlfriend and flew into the Hudson."

Now try the same equation with rickshaws, and the answer is always seven. Don't ask me why; I suck at math.

I'm done.

ARE YOU THERE, GOD? IT'S ME, JASON. AND I THINK YOU'RE A DICK

DEAR GOD, WHY?! WHY DID you have to take away Michael Jackson, your greatest treasure to the world? Why did you forsake him? Why did you let a 50-year-old child-molesting freak die, when so many children have not yet had their penises in his mouth?!

God, I am grief-stricken. Sure, people express grief in different ways: Some with tears; and others, like me, express it through dancing, clapping, and screaming, "Rot in Hell, you pasty-faced freak" at window-shaking intensity.

Wait. Michael Jackson is dead, right? I mean, he's looked like a worm-eaten, bloodless zombie for years. Somebody wave a picture of a naked Emmanuel Lewis in front of him…

No response? OK, he's definitely dead.

Anyway, God, even for you, this is a low blow—lower than the one Jacko gave to McCauley Caulkin.

As you know, I'm a stand-up comedian. And this is the worst thing you've done to me since you let George W. Bush leave office.

No, no! Don't go throwing Mark Sanford at me. It's too late for that.

Granted, your ways have always been a mystery, Big G. You've allowed Jacko to escape prison *and* you've allowed him to procreate, the latter of which, even by fans, was interpreted as a sign of the Apocalypse.

You've never sufficiently explained why you made that *Thriller* album such a hit. As far as I can tell, it's sole purpose was to launch the career of Weird Al Yankovic. But if it's comedy you want, Lord, why not just make millions of people suddenly love the taste of turd sandwiches?

Because that's what it felt like when I was twelve years old and *Thriller* came out. I was the only kid in junior high who, strangely, did not have a taste for aural diarrhea. My popularity, pathetic as it was, took an even greater beating— even worse than the beating Jacko gave to McCauley Caulkin's penis.

I realize that I'm not blameless for my pubescent ostracism, given the time in Civics class when I acted out every single dance move from Billy Joel's "Uptown Girl" video. But we can discuss another time why you made me retarded.

Later, of course, Jacko married Lisa Marie Presley, who admits that she had "marital relations" with her husband. Admit it: This caused even *you* to let loose with a celestial-sized whorf, which might explain the sudden emergence of Culture Club.

Even worse than the pederasty was Jacko's selling out the Beatles' catalog to advertisers, allowing diaper companies to even contemplate a slogan like, "All you need is Luvs." Remember that when he gets to Hell, and pile on another layer of hot, smoldering camel shit on his face, would ya?

Now that you've killed the mummified, baby-dangling, public masturbator, all I'm left with is this box of old Jacko jokes, like: "Jacko's youngest child is believed to have been conceived with a surrogate. Not the mother, of course—it was a surrogate penis."

Or: "Because of the criminal charges, Jacko will no longer invite young boys to Neverland. Now if he wants to meet young boys, he'll have to do it the old-fashioned way: At the confessional."

Of course, Jackson was never convicted of child molestation, which means we can all stop being so uptight about it. If we can't trust the same celebrity-ass-kissing juries that acquitted O. J. Simpson and Robert Blake, whom can you trust?

But now it's over, Lord. Twenty-five years of jokes about asexuality, boy-humping, and pigmentary liposuction—all out the window. Thanks a lot, God. Jackass.

And another thing: Way to go with Farrah Fawcett. You took a woman who at one time was considered the most beautiful woman in the world, made her a space case, and then killed her with asshole cancer? Dude, you are twisted.

In fact, you had her hook up with Ryan O'Neal, which means you gave her asshole cancer *twice*.

Charlie's Angels was the quintessential tits-and-ass TV show, so what do you do? You gave Kate Jackson titty cancer, and you give Farrah butt cancer.

What's next? Are you going to make flaming needles shoot out Jacklyn Smith's happy fun box? Cuz if you do, Lord, we're going to have a problem. Not as big a problem as Jacko's kids are going to have as memory-suppressing adults, but still…

And finally, you killed Ed McMahon. All I can say, God, is that you suck. Not as much as [*Editor's note: McCauley Caulkin penis joke redacted*].

I'm done.

HIM, AL FRANKEN:
THE FIRST 10 DAYS

WAS CONCERNED WHEN I SAW Al Franken's initial appearances as senator, as he insisted that he would put jokes aside and take the job seriously. This was clearly a sign of trouble, like watching someone trying to find meaning in a Michael Bay film.

I did not vote for Al Franken because I thought he would speak cogently about health care. I voted for him because I knew he could make something funny out of the words "bitch-slap" and "Sen. James Inhoffe."

So it was with relief when I saw Franken at the Sonia Sotomayor confirmation hearings, and he noted the irony of her wanting to become a prosecutor after watching *Perry Mason*, given that the prosecutor always lost.

She pointed out that the prosecutor in the show actually won one case. Franken asked her to name the episode, but she couldn't. "Didn't the White House prepare you for that?" Franken quipped.

Mind you, this isn't the raucous hilarity of making Jeff Sessions step on a bag of flaming dog poo, but as Senate hearings go, this is pretty funny.

But not if you ask the posters on YouTube, or CNN.com, or other websites that posted a clip of the hearings. These

123

viewers were not just unamused by the exchange: They were *angry*, as if Franken had written a scathing column on that dreamy pop god, Michael Jackson.

I don't say this with elitist, latte-drinking, liberal affectation; but generally speaking, the more right-wing the remarks were, the greater the spelling errors.

By that, I don't mean to suggest that these people are intellectually inferior or uneducated. What I mean is that they're just plain stupid.

And that's OK, because I really like using the indicator "[*sic*]," as you will see in this totally random posting that I selected for ridicule:

"democrats [*sic*] are making this a mockery!!! this [*sic*] is [*sic*] a supreme court [*sic*] justice [*sic*] and they are concerned with nancy drew [*sic*] novels and perry mason [*sic*]. Ladies and Gentelman [*sic*]....your 2009 Senate! Run by idiots, crooks and socialists!"

Now, I could point out that she's not yet a Supreme Court justice but a nominee. Or that the Senate is, in fact, run by morons, thieves, and Communists.

But if you're anything like me (and God help you if you are, badabing), you're probably struck by the fact that he can't capitalize "Perry Mason," or even the first word of a sentence, yet somehow manages to capitalize "Gentelman," calling into serious question the right-wing's passion for home Skooling.

Granted, I suppose it's true that we didn't need to know about her love for Nancy Drew novels as a child. Similarly, we could've been spared the recitation of Clarence Thomas's vast collection of his letters to *Penthouse.*

There are those who will find this criticism petty: After all, who expects to find intellectual discussion on a chat board, where one's political commentary *bona fides* consist solely of mobile fingers and a computer lab found at the library while wandering off the street to find a public restroom? To those people, I can say only this: F U DBAG GO 2 HLL + EAT SHT!!!! I H8 U!!!!!!!!

Another common thread in right-wing complaints about Franken is that having a comedian in the Senate is "an embarrassment." Of course. And there's absolutely no irony in the fact that the discussion of Minnesota's junior senator is being led by state residents whose literary skills are as polished as Joyce DeWitt's DUI mugshot.

Just to summarize: The U.S. Senate has Larry Craig, who is not gay but has gay bathroom sex; David Vitter, who was caught wearing a diaper with a hooker; and John Ensign, who had his mommy and daddy pay off his mistress, whose 19-year-old son was hired by the senator as an RNC policy analyst; and Robert Byrd, who was legally pronounced dead in 1997.

What does one have to do to be an "embarrassment" in that company? Besides, Republican senators Alan Simpson and Bob Dole were also known for telling jokes. And in the case of Dole, some were actually funny.

For example, there's Dole's famous gag in 1994, when he told his colleagues to kill any health care bill the president sends up, regardless of merit. The "Me, Al Franken" bit from *SNL* looks downright humble in contrast with Dole's king-sized bull-testicle waving.

Personally, I'd rather see more of the funny Al than the serious Al; but he's a senator now, so unfortunately, he won't be calling his critics big fat idiots.

That will have to be left up to *me*, Jason Johnson.

I'm done.

AN OVERDOSE OF DEMOCRACY AND BIRD POOP

NEED TO BEGIN WITH A semi-serious note to the recently convicted parents of the Wausau girl who died of untreated diabetes, because they thought they could cure her with the power of prayer: Are you yanking me?

Fervent prayer couldn't even get me laid in high school; why the hell did you think it could cure diabetes? Don't you think that if we could cure life-threatening diseases by dropping a coin in the celestial wishing well, someone would've tried that by now?

You do realize that we've had scores of Popes, and all but one of them has died? The last one had half the planet praying for him, and you know what? Didn't do him a hill of shit. And you, my religious zealot buddies, are not the Pope.

Of course, this emerged just before the case in Sleepy Eye, MN, where the mother tried to flee with her cancer-ridden child to Mexico, apparently believing that the Mayo Clinic was in Cancun.

No, actually, she wanted to treat her kid with alternative medicine, which—as NPR contributor David Rakoff can attest when he analyzed the alternative meds he bought for his own cancer–is made largely out of bird poop.

That's not a joke: It was bird poop. And I don't think it had to be Capistrano-swallow bird poop, either. She got have gotten any ol' bird in Sleepy Eye to poop in her kid's mouth. Granted, I don't know if birds die of cancer, but I do know that they die faster than most Popes.

Here's my deal with you faith-healing jackasses: If you want to pray your kid's cancer or diabetes away, start out praying for something small first. For example, pray that the Vikings win the Super Bowl. And if they win–congratulations! You've performed a miracle!

Until then, *DIAL FUCKING 911!*

I have no segue into my next subject, other than that it involves this collection of fucktards we collectively call "society."

We recently held an historic election. One that pitted progress against stagnation, reason over anti-intellectualism, and reforming health care over eating bird poop.

I'm talking about, of course, the election over the *Duluth News Tribune*'s cartoon page.

Needless to say, the same Duluth voters who said, "Hey, let's elect that Don Ness kid who works at the car wash as our mayor," blew it once again.

So they added *Beetle Bailey* and *Hagar the Horrible* to *Blondie*, *The Lockhorns*, and *Hi and Lois*? Yeah, this would be a great comics page, if this were 1973. For chrissake, they're still running *Peanuts*, and Charles Schulz has been dead for nine years!

Look, I understand that newspaper readers are about the age of the typical Bill O'Reilly viewer, which is to say, they were born on the scale of Earth's history somewhere to the left of the Pleistocene.

And old people don't understand humor. They don't get

the references in *Liberty Meadows, Pearls After Swine,* or *PVP.* They don't laugh at my "old people soiling their diapers" jokes. They didn't even grin when I said "fucktard."

But does this mean we have to riddle our comics page with shit like *The Wizard of Id,* which hasn't been funny since the first Reagan administration? Or *Funky Winkerbean,* which went from telling booger jokes to becoming an unending "very special episode" of *Family Matters*?

(I exclude from this list *Doonesbury,* which is still occasionally funny and still entertaining. I also excuse *Garfield,* because it spawed the Internet sensation *Garfield Minus Garfield,* which made me laugh so hard I squirted a little bit of Monday's lasagna dinner into my shorts.)

Worst of all, Duluth voters have failed to drive a spike through the heart of that brain-melting monstrosity: Bil Keane's bowl of humorless turds, *The Family Circus.*

I don't know how to explain this strip's continued existence other than a pact with Satan. And when Satan comes to Keane to collect his part of the bargain, I hope it involves sexual favors. There will be no justice in this universe if Keane doesn't end up with a mouthful of Satan testicles.

This strip is the Sarah Palin of comics: Moronic, vapid, shallow, and absolutely revered by glassy-eyed followers who refuse to acknowledge its inadequacy to be in the public arena. And while it's hated by the majority of rational Americans, we still cannot look away, because there's a bizarre attraction to its catastrophic failure, like watching the Nazis' heads melt in *Raiders of the Lost Ark.*

It just makes me want to barf and barf until I can barf no more. Hell, even their dog's name is Barfy!

So seriously, Duluth, as a city, I root for you. Individually, you can all eat bird poop and die.

I'm done.

THIS IS NOT ANOTHER COLUMN ABOUT FARTS* (*YES IT IS)

AS YOU NEW COLLEGE FRESHMEN begin classes, remember that our nation's future relies on your dedication to knowledge. For it is perhaps your generation that will reach Mars, cure cancers, achieve a new world order, and have sex with robots.

Or, as I hope will be the case, finally answer some of the mysteries of farts.

For example, I recently consumed a large quantity of tacos, and the resulting effluvium can be compared only to the odor of…burnt tacos. I realize that stomach acids are involved, but Frosted Flakes do not smell like burnt sugar toast, so what the hell? Am I digesting or barbequing back there? Did the Japanese plant a new anal hibachi in my rectum while I took my post-taco-engorging nap on the kitchen floor?

Speaking of Frosted Flakes, why don't they make your farts smell grrrrrr-reat? It's understood that smellier food will produce smellier farts, but shouldn't better-smelling foods give your farts just a hint of sugary goodness? Damn it, if I eat Honey-Nut Cheerios, I expect bees to go gay for my ass.

Farts should at least smell *better* after eating candy, but they instead reach what I call a fart's "odor ceiling." You can eat Starbursts until, well, you burst; but the coroner is not going to examine your splattered intestines and shout, "Mmmm! Smells like lime-on!"

Farts can go only from bad to worse. An exception to this rule is sauerkraut, which actually smells worse going down that it does coming out. In fact, it's probably worse than simply eating a big ol' plate of shit, although I don't recommend experimenting. If so, I think you will find a total lack of (1) friends, and (2) enough mouthwash on the entire planet.

Here's another mystery: Sometimes I have to fart before I get into my car. (That in itself is not a mystery; I've given up wondering why we have to fart while entering enclosed spaces. It's simply a law of nature.)

But sometimes I try to outwit the fart: I decide I'll fart *outside* the car before I enter the vehicle. Thus I let loose, perhaps knocking a bird or two out of the sky, and then leaping into the driver's seat before I can be ticketed for contributing to the accumulation of greenhouse gases.

This trick never works. The interior of the car *smells like a fart anyway*. How is this possible? I left the fart outside, in the open air, in perfect condition for matter dispersal. That's why wind exists: to disperse our own personal wind!

Did the fart somehow sneak in through a crack in the window–you know, out one crack and into another? Did it follow me inside, like a dog not wanting to leave its owner? That's all I need: a fart with abandonment issues.

Also, farting at the mall shouldn't be such a risky endeavor. You'd think with all the noise from the crowds–many of whom are probably farting at any given moment–that a good holiday sale should cover up a blast from the rear, even the kind that leaves gunpowder stains like an 1840s prospector playing with dynamite.

Yet even at its busiest hours, malls have acoustics that carry one's farts across the Dakotas. Plus, you're walking, which means the buttock separation makes it difficult to do the ol' fart-suppressing cheek-clench. You suddenly have empathy for priests who have to fart in the halls of the Vatican.

(Incidentally, I always wished that someone recorded Ethel Merman letting fly in an opera house, because I suspect it would be like standing in the middle of a rib-shaking thunderstorm. That's right: I *always* wished that. Some wish for gold or fame; me, I want to hear a fellow human being make a sound like a submarine dropping into the Grand Canyon. That's who I am.)

Sometimes, though, you have to let it go in the mall, and you try to let it out an ounce at a time. This inevitably results in an echoing, popping sound that you hope will sound to your companion as bubble wrap: *Poink!*

Companion: What was that?

You: Oh, I'm just cracking my knuckles! [*Crack knuckles again, hoping to imitate the popping sound.*]

Companion: Why do your knuckles smell like burnt tacos?

So again, college kids, I hope you can use your studies to answer these questions. But in the meantime, stay away from me until you've completed your research.

I'm done.

MY CLASSMATES ARE GRIZZLED OLD COOTS

TWENTY-YEAR REUNION WAS JUST HELD for the Class of '89, of which, I begrudgingly admit, I am a member. I did not attend the reunion party, and that appears to be just as well: According to the pictures of the reunion posted on Facebook, it was attended solely by a group of strange, unfamiliar old coots.

As I mentioned, I did not attend my high-school reunion, as I was busy doing the typical young person things, like being cool, looking sharp, and learning to eat with a spoon.

Besides, in high school, I was as popular as a case of herpes. In fact, I was actually less popular, because at least kids enjoyed *getting* herpes. Also, girls knew herpes existed.

The girls didn't respond to my dating attempts, apparently unswayed by my impressive collection of comicbooks and festering, golf-ball-sized zits. Similarly, the boys were unimpressed at my girlish wailing after they smashed my face open like a microwaved bag of pus.

So I was not exactly eager to meet up with this crowd again, considering that my dreams have crashed like a

Windows program and my career has all the sex appeal of Seth Rogan's unwashed thong.

But now I'm sorry I didn't go, because I could have had all those balding, overweight mummies entertain me with Civil War anecdotes. And I could laugh at them all, knowing that I was the only one still using his first set of dentures.

At the risk of sounding vain, I've got pictures to prove that I don't look all that different from my high school self. Sure, I've got man-boobs now; but they're young, pert man-boobs. I've got a few wrinkles, but none big enough to lose a Mars explorer in.

I don't dress any more fashionably, but I don't have to shop for shirts in the maternity section. My job isn't cool, but I don't have to leave a large, unaccounted-for gap on my resume to hide the prison time I spent for tax evasion, mail fraud, or for sexually assaulting a deer carcass.

This is quite a change from my ten-year reunion. I didn't attend that one, either, but I'd seen enough of my peers to know that they didn't look much different from their high-school selves, and they had spouses that were still attractive, while I was still living in my parents' basement with my invisible friend and chronic virginity.

It turns out, though, that hiding in my folks' basement saved me from having Life use my face as a football and morphing me into that walking cluster of age splotches that I used to call my classmates.

(It's worth adding that I wasn't even invited to my ten-year reunion. One of the organizers told me that they "couldn't find" me, even though I was still living at home, and she was the daughter of my mom's best friend. Hard to believe that they wouldn't want me there, in light of my almost preternatural ability to point out my classmates' faults.)

I felt a particular wave of Schadenfreude when I saw the photo of the girl who used to be among the hottest in my class. She was quite popular, which means that, in high school, she would give me a look like the one Nancy Pelosi gave Joe Wilson just before she chewed off his head and regurgitated it for her younglings.

But she now has as much of a chance of getting laid as I do. It's twenty years later, and this woman is Old, with a big fat "O." And she's Fat, with a big, fat Ass.

Seriously, she went from Cindy Crawford to William Howard Taft. Sure, there are guys out there who are chubby chasers—we call those guys "freaks," and rightly so. Meanwhile, there are lots of women who would sleep with me: We call them "hookers"—and rightly so.

I groan when I touch my toes, but I can at least *see* my toes. My hair is grayer, but the hair on my chest is *supposed* to be there. Maybe I couldn't pick up a girl in high school, but I could pick her up now…with a crane.

Is it wrong to mock the failures of my classmates, just because they've regressed into the loser I once was? Shouldn't I just take this opportunity to be thankful that I don't need liposuction, Botox, or a witness protection program?

Probably. But that would just get in the way of my maniacal laughter.

I'm done.

YOU WILL READ THIS
AND THEN SEND ME
ALL YOUR MONEY

DON'T KNOW WHAT DULUTH CHAMBER of Commerce frontman Dave Ross is pitching in those television ads that have begun airing on local TV stations. All I know is that he scares the living crap out of me, and I hit the fast-forward button before I add yet another brown spot to my undies.

I realize I'm in a bad position to mock other people's looks, but seriously: That bald head with the protruding brow; the skin pulled tight like a skull in decomposition; and the eerily dark, non-blinking eyes all remind me of that killer Yul Brenner cyborg in *Westworld*.

Now, this is the part where I would say, "I'm sure Dave Ross is a nice guy in person," but I really know nothing about him, other than that he must own a mirror somewhere in his house but *went on camera anyway*.

Unless, of course, he doesn't reflect in mirrors like some kind of soulless vampire, something that may well be a necessary qualification to work for the Duluth Chamber of Commerce.

Anyway, it makes me wonder how the public is expected

to respond to his ad when he looks like a villain from a Superman comic. I can only guess that his true cause is to make people run screaming from their homes into oncoming traffic.

This is not out of the realm of possibility. After all, the public has certainly been convinced to do dumber things, like betting on the Twins, voting Republican, or buying cat beds.

Yes, "cat beds." There really is such a thing. I don't know who buys these things, but presumably it's the same people whose pets were forced to dress as Batman this Halloween.

I need a cat bed like Obama needs another birth certificate. See, I already have a place for my cat to sleep. I call it *anywhere in my house.*

On my favorite chair. In the laundry basket. On the kitchen table. On the refrigerator. On the ceiling fan. On my face when I'm trying to sleep.

Does this sound familiar to you cat owners? "You're lucky you're cute or I'd drown you!"

Kidding, of course. That's something you should say only to your children.

I realize that persuading people to buy things they don't need is essential to the economy. If consumers were smart, there'd be no singing fish, snuggies, collectable dinner plates, Rob Schneider films, or Catholicism.

But I've often wondered how people get persuaded into doing really stupid things. For example, I often hear stories of how a voice in a guy's head talked him into cleaving his family with an axe, burn their bodies in a trash can, and then, tragically, buy a painted dinner plate and expect it to appreciate in value.

I'm thinking that voice has got to be a really smooth

talker. I always wonder why it didn't just get a job on QVC. At least there seems to be money in that.

To be fair, not all evil voices are killers. Many are relatively common Joes, making their living as Fox News political pundits.

But inner voices never seem to offer practical advice, like "Bend your knees more when you swing," or "Put less mayonnaise on your nachos," or "Why not use that $30 as toilet paper instead of buying a stupid cat bed? At least then it won't go to waste."

I know an inner voice could never talk me into committing murder. It's not that I'm not evil enough, mind you. I'm just really bad at following directions.

Voice: Kill your neighbor.

Me: Now? *Fat Camp* is on.

Voice: You've watched this episode a thousand times. Now kill your neighbor.

Me: I'll do it during the commercial break.

Voice: That's what you said the last seven times, and all you did was go to the freezer and stuff boxes of pudding pops down your bloated gullet.

Me: Why do you want to kill Bob, anyway? Just because his snot whistles when he laughs?

Voice: Yes, but actually, I was referring to that 80-year-old crone next door who fetches her paper wearing a see-through bathrobe. Now, get a chainsaw–

Me: I can't start a chainsaw.

Voice: Are you [*censored*] serious?! All you do is pull a damn cord!

Me: No, there's also a choke-thingy, too, like the lawnmower. I don't even know what a choke-thingy does. All I know is that I haven't mowed my lawn in eight months.

That, by the way, is sad but true. Seriously, I don't know how many lives have been spared simply because I lack the technical know-how to operate a woodchipper. And I've probably saved a few more lives after I stopped making ads for the Duluth Chamber of Commerce.

I'm done.

PRESIDENT-ELECT TIM PAWLENTY'S 2012 VICTORY SPEECH, AND OTHER CRAP THAT'LL NEVER HAPPEN

M Y FELLOW AMERICANS, I HAVE just gotten off the phone with President Biden. [*Boos from the audience.*] Now, now, there's no place for that. Seriously, it was a four-hour phone call, and we really don't have time. I'm missing Craig Ferguson.

He was gracious enough to give me some advice: "Don't judge a book by its cover, or who you will love by your lover."

I said, "Mr. President, you plagiarized that from Aerosmith's 'Dude Looks Like a Lady,'" but he just rambled on about his once having Woodrow Wilson's personal email.

I would like to thank my family, my supporters, and of course, Jesus. For was it not Jesus' hand that led us to the truth about the former President Obama, whose true birth certificate revealed him to have been born in Kenya under the name Bert O'Hara, and who now runs the pro-Stalinistic, militant Muslim wing of ACORN? Stand up and take a bow, Jesus.

[*Jesus, who looks conspicuously like Matt Drudge in a bathrobe and fake beard, waves to the cheering crowd.*]

And Jesus also led us to the *real* Barack Obama, whose birth was the one that was announced in the Hawaiian newspapers in 1962, and who is now an insurance adjuster from Brule, WI. But you know him better as our campaign mascot, Barack the Insurance Guy!

[*Cheers as the real Barack Obama, a white guy with a bald spot and a plaid shirt, waves to the crowd. The cheers go on for ten minutes.*]

Their help, and with the help of the American people, have made me your next president!

[*Crickets.*]

Ahem. People said this night couldn't happen. They said I couldn't be president if I ran on my zero accomplishments as governor, an office I won twice by plurality. But they were wrong about Bert O'Hara's birth certificate, and they were wrong about us!

Sure, our campaign caught a few lucky breaks: Sarah Palin lost Iowa to a moose carcass. Mitt Romney became so insubstantial that he dissipated into thin air. And Mike Huckabee married a dog.

Then Ron Paul went certifiably nuts and killed Charlie Crist with a spoon; Lindsay Graham was careless enough to bad-mouth my running mate, Glenn Beck; Rudy Giuliani didn't start campaigning until last Thursday; and Haley Barbour's a fat guy.

Bobby Jindahl turned out to be a chick. Newt Gingrich turned out to be, well, Newt Gingrich. And the Constitution says that Carrie Prejean is too young to be president. Plus, she's a dude.

And to be honest, our campaign did get a bit of a boost from the mass hypnosis; the collective amnesia in my home state due to toxic drinking water; massive voter fraud; voter error; and occasionally wearing a mask and telling stupid people that I was one of the Jonas Brothers.

And then there was the Global-warming Flood of 2011, which took out the East and West Coasts. We should probably have a moment of silence or something, but lord, it's half past midnight, and Barack the Insurance Guy is lapsing into a whiskey-induced coma.

I'm done. God bless America, all remaining 22 states.

YOU WON'T UNDERSTAND YOUR DOG, AND OTHER 2010 PREDICTIONS

FOR 2010, I RESOLVE NOT to resort to writing columns of lists. They are intellectually and comedically lazy, like people who make jokes about Tiger Woods' mistresses using "putter," "line drive," and "hole-in-one" as double entendres.

However, that's for 2010. In the meantime, here's another intellectually and comedically lazy list of my 2010 predictions:

*The world will not end, but it will seem like it when Playgirl begins featuring an ass-shaking Tom DeLay.

*President Obama, after having successfully prevented torture prosecutions and blocking freedom of information acts, completes his transition into Bush by spitting when he talks, forgetting how to open doors, and giving the Pope the nickname, "Ol' Pointy Hat."

*The Democrats will lose both houses of Congress during the midterms, losing even more Senate seats than were up for election. The majority Republican caucus will not even take roll call before someone utters, "Who the hell let Joe Lieberman in here?"

*Having successfully killed health care reform, Big Pharma will tell Congress to pass a bill requiring congressmen to dance! Dance, we say! It will get rare bipartisan support.

*A celebrity will have a sex scandal which will receive such non-stop news coverage that Americans will be completely unaware of other major news stories, such as the fact that dogs have suddenly begun talking in fluent Portuguese.

*Hey, you know that city of Boise, Idaho? Yeah, don't get to used to it. Just sayin'.

*The Salahis' new reality show will come to a fortuitous conclusion when that balloon-boy dad launches them into the troposphere.

*Victoria's Secret model Aurelia Gliwski will develop an intense passion for overweight, underemployed English majors who work for small alternative newspapers.

*Jason Johnson will release his next book, *Here's Another Damn Book That No One Will Read*. Unlike that last prediction, the book title will be painfully true.

*In order to cut costs, the postal service will cease delivery during golf season. No one will notice.

*Someday you will have kids and they will turn out just like you and then you will be sorry!

*A computer company will manufacture something, and *you must have it*, because the media will tell you that it is *vitally important to your well-being*, and you will spend *thousands of dollars on it*, and you will not have a *goddamn clue* what it does.

*Rick Warren will be found powder-nosed and naked

with Ted Haggard. Given gay-bashers' predilection for boinging other dudes, this is hardly a prediction, which is why I'm letting you have this one on the house.

*Yoko Ono will be doused in water and melt away. Actually, this is less of a prediction and more of a fervent hope.

*I haven't seen the new Iron Man flick yet, but some dude sent me a clip and it's gonna ROCK!! I give it FIVE STARS!!!! (This prediction courtesy of a 15-year-old Amazon.com reviewer.)

*Cerulean will be the new azure.

*Adam Lambert will have a hit song. You won't understand why.

*Following the revelation of sexy text messages between Minnesota's senators, the word "franken" will enter the vocabulary as a vulgar sex term.

*Capricorn: Romance is in your future. Unfortunately, it will involve a homeless man who offers to kiss you in exchange for shaving his back.

*Spongebob Squarepants will hit puberty. Episodes will involve his struggles with foam-rubber acne and girls' calling him "Nothing-Down-There"-Pants.

*A meteor will not strike the Earth. However, your roommate will be cold-cocked by a beer bottle for not shutting up about Linux.

*The biggest blockbuster of the 2010 summer movie season? A Donny Osmund bio-pic.

*Jesus will return. He will hear Sarah Palin refer to him as her savior, and he will throw up.

*Michele Bachmann will say something crazy; a sports star will have a drug scandal; and the public will attach too much relevance to a reality TV show.

Finally, you will get older but no wiser. In fact, you're expected to get a little stupider following a glue-sniffing bender.

You're welcome.

PEOPLE: FULLA CRAP, AS USUAL

OFTEN WEAR A BUTTON ON my chest that reads, "Lucifer for Congress." For those of you not paying attention, it is the name of one of the cartoons in the *Zenith City Weekly*, the newspaper for whom I work. It's partly a sign of support for my hometown paper, but mainly I wear it simply because I like decorating my nipples.

Seriously, if you're not leasing your pectorals to advertisers, you may as well flush huge wads of cash down the toilet.

In any case, I'm often stopped by passers-by who remark, "Lucifer for Congress? Isn't that what we have now?"

And I always respond, "Wow, you are the *first person* to ever think of that line! No, really, I'm not being sarcastic! You're just as witty and clever as you think you are." Then I yelp in pain, having had my button forcibly torn from my areola.

But my smart-assery is justified. Because these would-be comedians are confusing Satan with a king of Babylon, a mistake easily made if one has the IQ of a coconut, a doormat, or Ann Coulter.

Biblically speaking, "Lucifer" does not mean "Satan." It means "light-bearer" and only became to mean "Satan" through a mistranslation by St. Jerome, whom the other saints nicknamed, "Ol' Saint Can't-Translate-for-Shit."

Of course, many people who make this mistake are probably Christian. And it's pointless to explain that Christians don't understand Christianity—that ship sailed about 2000 years ago. But here's some crap I can shovel:

*Lincoln did not have a secretary named Kennedy. This is supposed to be one of those creepy coincidences between Lincoln and JFK, but all of Lincoln's secretaries were men, and none were named Kennedy. However, Lincoln did receive an erotic rendition of "Happy Birthday Mr. President" from Salmon P. Chase, which all in attendance agreed was "sorta gross."

*America was not named after Amerigo Vespucci. This answers the question asked by every 5th grader, "Why isn't America named Vespuccica?" The answer is because, much like the stories of your alcohol-free conception, the Vespucci story is a damn lie.

America was instead named after the wealthy Welsh businessman and John Cabot's patron, Richard Amyrik, who had a Donald-Trump-like quality to stamp his name on anything he could get his hands on, like merchant ships, a new continent, or Carrie Prejean's breasts.

At this point, the 5th graders ask, "Then why isn't it spelled 'Amyrika'?" And the answer is: Shut the hell up, you pre-pubescent pain in the ass.

*Washington was the first president of the United States. Why do I even have to address this? Because some will tell you that Washington was not the first president, as there were 14 previous presidents of the Continental Congress—proving that "some" has been eating expired pain medication they found on the bathroom floor at Arby's.

President of the Continental Congress was a different

job with different duties and different powers. Before Washington, the States were functioning under the Articles of Confederation, which I believe is fancy-pants talk for "anarchy," a.k.a., "Ron Paul's Wet Dreamland."

This is why Washington gets put on the front of the dollar bill, while the back is given to the first "President of the United States in Congress Assembled," who was named, of course, John Creepy Eye Over Pyramid.

Howard Dean did not lose the 2004 nomination because of the "Dean Scream." It is unfathomable that people get this wrong, especially when it was a mere six years ago, when most political observers were presumably alive and sentient, with the possible exception of Sarah Palin.

Yet this lie is often promulgated by political pundits, whose qualifications apparently do not consist of understanding politics, reading a calendar, or, in Karl Rove's case, not making viewers puke onto their TV trays.

However, those with a basic understanding of the concept of "time" will realize that the "Dean Scream" occurred *after* he lost Iowa. In New Hampshire, Dean was already losing ground against his chief opponent, John "Ohio Is a State I'll Never" Kerry, and it was the Kerry's dual victories in those key states that secured his nomination. Well, that and his overpowering charisma.

No one expects the Spanish Inquisition. Not true. In 1486, a gay, atheist, pot-smoking dildo salesman kinda saw it coming.

Carl Sagan did not say "billions and billions." At least, he didn't say it until much later, and never in a scientific context. The phrase came from a Sagan impression by Johnny Carson. It is unclear if Sagan ever uttered the other phrase attributed to him, "Stephen Hawking can stick it up his robotic, paralyzed wormhole."

   *U2's *The Joshua Tree* **is an overrated piece of crap.** Fortunately, the only people who think otherwise are Bono and your college roommate who still wears a Night Ranger T-shirt and laughs at reruns of *Alf.*

   I'm done.

MASSIVE HUMAN TRAGEDY = COMEDY GOLD

"Political odd couple is born as Bush embraces 'step-brother' Clinton"—San Francisco Chronicle, **January 17, 2010**

HILLARY CLINTON: Bill, former president Bush, I appreciate your joining together to coordinate relief efforts her in Haiti after this devastating earthquake.

GEORGE W. BUSH: Kuarnate.

HC: Coordinate.

W: Quarternate.

HC: Never mind. Just make sure the supplies get where they're supposed to go.

W: I don't like it here! It's messy, crumbly, and stinky! It's stupid and no one knows what's going on!

HC: Now you know how *we* felt for eight years. Bill, show him what to do.

BILL CLINTON: Sorry, doll, but I gotta jaunt over to the Dominican Republic and meet with some topless—I mean, top heads of state. Won't be back till 2 AM.

HC: You'll be back for dinner at six.

BC: How about 12 midnight?

HC: Jesus Christ, it's easier to negotiate with Ahmadinejad.

By the way, people here are scrambling for clean water. Where the hell'd you get those apple schnapps?!

BC: I know a guy who knows a guy.

W: Hey, I know a guy, too! A guy who runs a disaster management company! Maybe he can help us!

HC: Sounds like someone we want on our team. What's his name?

W: Michael Brown.

[*Author's note: Michael "Heckofajob" Brownie's post-Katrina employment status was, for a time, literally true. Seriously. We couldn't make this crap up. Well, we could, but we're not that evil.*]

HC: Wait, wait. I wasn't ready for that. [*Pours herself a large glass of apple schnapps.*] What was that name again? [*Takes huge gulp.*]

W: Michael Brown!

HC: [*Executes flawless, hilarious spit-take onto Bill's leisure suit.*]

BC: Ahhh! Hillary, I'm not Quinn's father!

HC: You're off the hook on that one, Bill. John Edwards has already admitted paternity.

W: Puhturdiddy. [*Giggles.*]

BC: Oh, thank God for that! Cuz you know I had sex with that woman Rielle Hunter, too, right?

HC: [*Sighs.*] Yes, Bill, I know.

BC: Yeah, I totally tapped that hot blonde videographer ass. Got the tapes somewhere.

W: They're hot.

BC: Thanks, bro!

HC: Yes, I know about the tapes. As clearly spelled out in the new book on the 2008 election, *Game Change* by John Heilemann and Mark Halperin–the same book in which we learned the shocking revelation that an elderly white guy from Arizona still uses the word "Negro"–my campaign staff concluded that you were indeed having an affair.

W: I don't like books. Well, maybe that one by Sarah Palin.

BC: Tapped that.

HC: Bill!

BC: What! You were there!

W: Brother, you are a *dawg*!

BC: And you're the best step-brother a guy could have! C'm here, you! [*Puts W in a headlock and gives fistrub on his head.*]

ROGER CLINTON: Hey, what about me?

HC: Roger? Have you been here this whole time?

BC: You know this guy?

RC: [*Turns to audience*] That's my Bubba!
[*Collective laugh. End credits.*]

HAPPY VALENTINES DAY!
NOW GO SCREW A ROBOT

N THE 1950S, IF SUPERMAN and Clark Kent had to appear in public together, he would simply reach into his closet and pull out a robot duplicate of himself. This robot would always fool Lois Lane, because, as he learned from his clever eyeglasses disguise, Lois was dumber than dirt.

It was never explained how Superman made these robots on a reporter's salary. Or why he didn't go into a more lucrative profession, like—oh, I don't know—ROBOTICS.

Meanwhile, Lois would keep rejecting Clark's advances, even though he looked a lot like her dream boy Superman, shared her interest in journalism, and appeared to be one hell of a handyman.

But as a kid, I was plagued with another question: Why didn't Superman just make a Lois Lane robot and fuck *that*? Wouldn't that be preferable to saving her shallow, clumsy ass every twenty minutes?

It was questions like this that made me different from the other kids.

But now I know I worried for nothing, thanks to Roxxxy the sexbot and the good people at TrueCompanion.com. Further proof—as if more was needed after online sex and sexting—that science makes its greatest strides when it's finding new ways to get our rocks off.

Looking at the pictures of Roxxxy on the website, it is clear that she is quite the stunner. She looks a lot like Rosanna Arquette if Arquette were a Cro-Magnon. And a dude. And had breasts only slightly more realistic than Tara Reid's.

As for her personality, inventor Douglas Hines says he modeled her after a friend who was lost in the 9/11 attacks. It's not clear if the deceased's personality was (actual personality choices from the website) "Wild Wendy," "Mature Martha," or "S & M Susan." There's also a personality choice creepily named "Young Yoko," because nothing gets one in the mood than the thought of a conniving, screeching, bat-faced ex-Beatle wife.

(In fact, if you watch the demonstration of the sexbot on YouTube, the Yoko name is dropped, and the sexbot says—I am not kidding—"I used to have a name, but it was decided at the last minute that it was too creepy for the trade show demonstration." At last, good taste prevails.)

And then there's "Frigid Farrah," a personality that, according to the website, "will not be... appreciative" to your touching her private parts. In other words, men can now pay seven grand for a sexbot that will treat him like every other woman on the planet.

Again, it's unclear which personality was Hines' deceased friend. But the fact that his friend will be ridden by hundreds of horny losers is tribute enough. Fortunately, the 9/11 attacks apparently didn't kill any of his farm animals.

But in case you forget the tragic origin of the sexbot, you can, as the demonstration video shows, program her to describe her death in the Twin Towers. You can also program her to have a man's voice (not kidding) that will cry (again, not kidding), "I am trapped in Hell. Please kill me." If you're not turned on by then, well, you must be a Frigid Farrah.

But that's not the extent of Roxxxy's dirty talk. Here is an actual quote: "You have a nice wiener." Yes, apparently one of her personalities is a seven-year-old.

Roxxxy is also designed to be a swinger. The website boasts that you can download your friend's sexbot's personality, which "is the same as wife or girlfriend swapping without any of the social issues or sexual disease related concerns!"

Yes, because when you swap girlfriends, what you want is to screw the *same woman* who no longer knows who the hell you are. Anyway, with my luck, I'd accidentally download a computer virus that gives me virtual crabs.

Now I know what you men are asking: Can she talk about soccer? I know you're asking this, because the question appears in the "Frequently Asked Questions" section. Says Hines: "Yes, she can talk about soccer."

Ka-CHING!

Of course, the fact that customers are frequently asking this question also answers the question of why they are not sleeping with a real woman.

As for you ladies, by now you're probably asking, "Are you men looking to replace real women?"

Ha ha ha! Ah, you ladies with your stupid, babbling questions! That's just one of the reasons we replaced you long ago with inflatable dolls.

In fact, the sexbots are not built to replace women, but the inflatable women, who, while bargain priced, make loud uncomfortable farting noises and have that O-shaped mouth that makes them look surprised all the time. As if a guy never before asked her to talk about soccer.

And yes, there is a male sexbot, Rocky, in the works, but he's not yet commercially available. And even when he is, he still won't be emotionally available. Am I right, ladies? Badaboom.

I'm done.

BLACKS AND GAYS AND TRANSVESTITES, OH MY!

LAST MONTH WAS BLACK HISTORY Month, in which schoolchildren are drilled about MLK, Harriet Tubman, and Rosa Parks, because those are the only black people that suburban white teachers know.

Some teachers attempted to add Barack Obama to the list of notable black personages, until Fox News wisely pointed out that this would be indoctrination, and you know who else does that? Why, none other than Adolph Pol Pot Stalin Hussein bin Laden, that's who!

And while every child should know about Harriet Tubman, let's be honest: By the third week, that Underground Railroad crap gets old. By the end of the month, teachers get desperate for different black leaders, until finally they resort to teaching about Lewis Black, the Black-Eyed Peas, AC/DC's *Back in Black*, and Michael Jackson's original face.

That's where three Los Angeles school teachers come in. In an effort to punch up the celebration, they decided to include a double murderer, a wife beater, and a transvestite. So for the first time since its inception, we had a Black History Month that educational *and* a boatload of fun, the kind that can be brought about only by racial tension and cross-dressing.

It seems the three white teachers wanted to include O.J. Simpson, Dennis Rodman, and RuPaul. Naturally, parents were outraged. I mean, really: *RuPaul*?!

O.J. and Rodman are sports legends! Why would they get lumped into the same category as RuPaul, a transvestite whose only accomplishments are singing, dancing, modeling, and providing masturbation material to both genders? What were they thinking?!

Fortunately, civil rights advocates recognize that everyone deserves respect, except for men who wear dresses. Transvestites are the worst of both sexes: They're ugly like men, and they're bad drivers like women, which is why they need to be chauffeured by Eddie Murphy.

I was also initially confused by the inclusion of wife-slapper Dennis Rodman, who has also been known to wear a dress, until I realized that the teachers wanted to honor him for a different accomplishment–namely, banging Carmen Electra.

Otherwise, who would want to honor a gaudily dressed, unintelligible, flaming narcissist, who's a lousy husband to boot? But enough about Rudy Giuliani.

This racial brouhaha arises while another controversy brews in Arkansas, where the Zeta Tau Alpha sorority won a collegiate step-dancing contest. Apparently, they were cheered when they performed but booed when they won, because it turned out… they were white. Worse yet, they were transvestites.

But the biggest complaint is that the white girls were "stealing" step-dancing from the black teams, much like white people stole rock music, street idioms, and, of course, Michael Jackson. But this overlooks all the things that black people stole from whites, such as our wallets and car stereos.

Ha ha ha! See what I did? I exposed the silliness of the stereotype that black people steal by making a little joke about it. We all know that most crimes are, in truth, committed by Mexicans.

Actually, blacks did steal one thing that was clearly the sole property of whites; and that thing is, of course, the presidency. And Dennis Rodman's ten-day-marriage is a tradition that he stole from Larry King, who invented the practice back in 1789.

Speaking of Larry King, cross-dressing, and dancing, I need to address the sexual harrassment charges against congressman Eric "Tickle-Me" Massa, a former Naval officer who was apparently also the sailor for the Village People.

King asked Massa if he were gay, and Massa responded by saying that King should "ask the tens of thousands of men I served with in the Navy." Well, someone asked them, and their answer: Ohhhh yeah. He is *so* gay. Like, Larry Craig doing a reach-around on Mark Foley-gay.

On one occasion, Massa admits to walking in on a fellow sailor masturbating and asked, "Let me know if you need any help with that." By the way, here's a tip: If another dude helps you masturbate, it's no longer masturbation.

Fittingly, this revelation comes up (so to speak) at a time when the military seems poised to overturn the ban on gays in the military. That is, until John "Palin Sure Seemed Like a Good Idea at the Time" McCain held up a list of over a thousand military personnel who opposed the idea. And, of course, they were all transvestites.

No, kidding. However, the list seems to be composed of three groups of people: (1) Those who truly believe in the gay ban; (2) those who–strange as it may seem, given their names on the list–do *not* believe that gays should be banned from the military.

The third group is perhaps the most intriguing: They're dead. Yes, apparently Stonewall Jackson and Robert E. Lee had all the tickle-fighting and masturbation assistance they could handle. Even though they were transvestites.

I'm done.

PRESENTING: ALL THE NEXT GOVERNORS OF MINNESOTA!

MN STATE SENATOR TOM BAKK recently announced his departure from the 2010 gubernatorial race. This caused cries of anguish across the state, all asking the same burning question: "Tom who did what, now?"

The race became wide open after Tim Pawlenty announced that he would not be seeking re-election, choosing instead to spend more time cutting health services to his family.

By 2011, the Democrats will have been out of power for twenty years. This has resulted in their eyeing the governor's office like Tiger Woods eyes cocktail waitresses.

The last time a Democrat owned the seat, Alan Parsons still had a Project, the Soviet Union had only recently collapsed, and Ann Coulter was still mildly pretty, before her skin congealed into the *Texas Chainsaw Massacre*'s Leatherface.

So even without the presence of Tom Bakk, there are plenty of Democratic candidates to bore the crap out of you before finding a new way to lose. Here, as a public service, we offer the menu:

Matt Entenza: Former House minority leader and

current low-vote getter. Came into prominence after his contemplated run for attorney general, when it was revealed that he hired a Chicago crime boss to rough up his political opponents. Or he hired opposition research to dig up Mike Hatch's parking tickets. Or he hired a consulting firm to tell him what the hell an attorney general does all day. Tomato, tomahto.

Tom Rukavina: Hey, remember that DUI he got back in 2004? Tom's counting on the fact that you won't, possibly because you were too wasted in his back seat to notice. To be fair, having a few stiff drinks is the only way new sports arenas start to look like a good idea.

R.T. Rybak: Mayor of Minneapolis and probably every social studies teacher you ever had. He was endorsed by Duluth mayor Don Ness but shows his political stamina by continuing to run anyway. His campaign began inauspiciously when it was revealed that "R.T." was short for "Really Terrible at Running for Governor."

Margaret Anderson Kelliher: Speaker of the MN House, and isn't that adorable? It's cute the way women try to do man stuff, like lead the state. Precious! Unfortunately, state law dictates that your name can't be so long that it takes 4% of the state budget just to make the nameplate for your desk.

Steve Kelley: Of all the candidates, only Kelley shows the promise of taking back the governor's seat for the Democrats. Smart, politically savvy, and having male genitalia, Kelley is a state senator and a man of destiny–

Aaaaaand…he just dropped out. I guess his destiny was to be unelectable. Moving on.

John Marty: State senator and all-around nice guy, Marty ran for governor in 1994, getting trounced so badly by Arne Carlson that he still has Arne's bootprint across his forehead, as well as what many political analysts lovingly call "Loser Stink."

He also has an unfortunate name, which conjures up the image of him diving into a time-traveling Delorean while wearing a life preserver.

Mark Dayton: Oh boy. Really? Isn't this the guy who served only one term in the U.S. Senate because he became less popular than a 50-year-old hooker with visible herpes? Didn't he admit that he deserved an "F" grade as senator? Is he hoping that people will elect him just so they can have a bumper sticker that says, "My Governor Could Get Thrashed by Your Honor Student"?

Susan Gaertner: Mmmmm... No.

Paul Thissen: Even his staff doesn't know who this guy is. All his spokesman could tell me is that they take orders from a creepy electronic voice over the phone. He was about to say more but was shot through the heart by a limping man in a trenchcoat who escaped into the darkness, taking the secret of Thissen's gubernatorial run with him.

Why the limping man didn't shoot *me* instead, I'll never know. Mind you, I'm not complaining; it's just that he must have spent a lot of time and money training this guy to be his spokesman, and I was just as much in the line of fire, so... Weird.

Anyway, that's the cast of characters on the Democratic gubernatorial race. If none of them appeal to you, you can vote for the same person you voted for last time: Donald Duck. And he probably stands a better chance of winning.

I'm done.

AN IMMODEST PROPOSAL FOR DULUTH'S LAMPPOST HISTORY MONTH

'VE OFTEN BEEN CYNICAL OF the South's love of "tradition," especially when said tradition is racist, violent, or started only seven minutes ago.

Lately, though, I've come to recognize the beauty of one of their traditions: selective memory. For example, I personally choose to remember only the times in high school when I was really cool, which is why I remember nothing about the second Reagan administration.

Recently, Virgina governor and Grecian hair formula model Bob McDonnell issued a proclamation celebrating Confederate History Month, which declared:

*Armed insurrection, despite the treason and bloodshed, is really wicked cool.

*The Confederacy is a part of Virginia's heritage and deserves at least as much recognition as Tennessee's Massive Indian Genocide Month.

*Grits be tasty.

*Slavery? What is this slavery of which you speak?

Yes, you can now celebrate armed insurrection guilt free, thanks to good ol' Southern revisionist boys, the same people who put Jefferson Davis on par with Abe Lincoln in Texan schoolbooks, and who replaced teaching evolution in the schools with non-stop re-reruns of *The Dukes of Hazzard*.

Revisionists point out that the Civil War was fought for reasons other than slavery, which is absolutely true. It was actually about "states' rights"–specifically, the right to have poll taxes, literacy tests for voting, separate drinking fountains, and the occasional human being sold as cattle.

McDonnell eventually apologized, pointing out that he excluded any mention of slavery to focus on what was "important to Virginians," which perhaps also explains his following proclamation celebrating Lady Gaga's cleavage.

Fortunately, Mississippi governor Haley Barbour wouldn't be cowed by such liberal carping about slavery, telling CNN about the controversy: "To me, it's a sort of a feeling that it's a nit, that it is not significant, that it's… trying to make a big deal out of something [that] doesn't amount to diddly."

Yes! The rotund, tone-deaf, redneck governor of Mississippi–the same state that celebrates Robert E. Lee Day on the same day of MLK's birthday–is absolutely correct! It *is* just a nit!

At least, I think it is. To be honest, I had to look "nit" up in the dictionary. Apparently, it's the egg of a louse. Coincidentally, I then looked up "louse" and found Haley Barbour.

As every Duluth resident knows, we have our own racist past to sweep casually under the rug. In 1920, Duluthians stormed the jailhouse and lynched three black men accused of raping a white woman and, perhaps worse, proposing an overhaul of the health care system.

But hey, if we learned anything from Bob McDonnell and Haley Barbour, it's that we don't have to focus on the negative! Well, that, and the fact that one can apparently become the governor of an entire state without having a conscience, a grasp of history, or an aversion to high fructose corn syrup.

So let's not think of the 1920 lynchings as the cold-blooded murder of three innocent black men. Rather, consider it part of Minnesota's heritage of enjoying outdoor communal activities and defending the great American value of majority rules!

In fact, when discussing the event, it's perhaps best if we don't mention the hanging victims as all, instead focusing on, as Bob McDonnell suggests, what is "important to Duluthians," i.e., the sturdiness of Duluth's lampposts, built with good ol'-fashioned Duluthian know-how.

And could Duluthians ever tie knots? Please!

That is why I propose that Duluth mayor Don Ness declare June as Lamppost History Month. And should there be any complaints from the bleeding hearts–or "lenghty necks," as we traditionalists call them–just remember that we're obligated to honor our ancestors, no matter what, simply because they had sex with our grandmas.

Let us commence with the altering of history books, to portray our ancestors as wide-eyed idealists who freed blacks from the confines of their prison cells. It could almost be called "Lincolnesque," if Lincoln hadn't been such a pussy.

And to think, we have Haley Barbour to thank for giving us a new outlook on what had previously been a shameful chapter in Duluth history. In fact, I think that's a good word for it: Barbourism. Yeah, I like that: Haley the Barbourian. Any similarity to actual barbarism is strictly intentional.

I'm done.

SOMETHING TO TALK ABOUT WHILE HANGING AROUND THE JUNIOR HIGH SCHOOL

So Larry King is having marital troubles because of alleged infidelity. Man, he has got to be one smooth talker. The guy's been married eight times and has been medically dead for the last three of them.

Seriously, John McCain looks at King and thinks, "That guy is *old*." I realize that he's rich and famous, but it's still unsettling that he gets more tail than I do, when he's more of a walking skeleton than Nicole Richie and has only slightly bigger breasts.

Geriatric sex is often frowned upon by society, and rightly so. The idea is so disgusting, I'd rather have old people driving. I'd actually feel safer with Larry King getting behind the wheel of car than getting behind Betty White.

But curiously, it gets far less scorn than an underaged teens have sex, even though that's what underaged teens are built for, other than to be walking, shopaholic pimple factories.

Mind you, when I condone sex with minors, I'm not talking about the Catholic Church, who recently "forgave" the Beatles for the "bigger-than-Jesus" flap, proving that the Vatican has gone from fucking little boys to fucking with our heads.

Ringo summed it well by pointing out that the Vatican has far bigger things with which to make amends, which in turn prompted the church to point out that their forgiveness does not extend to Ringo's cover of "Only You."

But I digress. Recently, NY Giants linebacker Lawrence Taylor was charged with two victimless crimes: (1) having sex with a 16-year-old, and (2) having sex for cash–which I believe also describes at least half of Hugh Hefner's marriages.

I've talked about the injustice of statutory rape laws before, and I hasten to add that just because I *want* to have sex with teenage girls, it doesn't mean that I *could* have sex with teenage girls, who see me as a creepy old guy, largely because I want to have sex with teenage girls.

But every time I broach the subject, someone has to ask me, "What if it was *your* daughter?!"

First of all, if it were my daughter, I would complain to the escort service. Asking for a hooker and getting your own daughter is a serious breach of customer-pimp etiquette. I mean, dude, my own daughter? You don't think I've already tapped *that* ass?

Secondly, to have a daughter, I'd have to have sex, which, as I've said, is highly unlikely, unless I had Lawrence Taylor's bank account or was involved in prison rape.

In any case, for most of human history, females were married almost as soon as they hit puberty, making everyone here a descendant of a statutory rapist. You're only reading this because your great-great-great-great-grandpa didn't give two shits about New York's penal code. Plus, your great-great-great-great-grandma was a bit of a slut.

Granted, mores have changed, but human biology has

not. We're not above marketing our daughters as trollops, as evidenced by recent Miley Cyrus videos.

In fact, I recently saw a panel discussion that asked, "Is the new Miley Cyrus video too hot?"–which seems to indicate that our barrel of intelligent questions has run dry. Nobody can be "too hot." Although, contrary to legend, it is possible to be too thin or too rich (I'm looking at *you*, Kate Moss and Bernie Madoff!).

Besides, Miley Cyrus's hotness will always be held in check by the thought of her dad's boner- shrinking "Achy Breaky Heart." Or just remembering the fact that Larry King tapped that.

I'm done.

JASON JOHNSON HAS THE SUCKIEST FACEBOOK PAGE

JASON **J**OHNSON HAS DECIDED TO start a Facebook page. If my MySpace page is anything to go by, most of my friends will be relatives, bands looking to promote their shitty indie act, or hot babes spamming me with ads for their porn sites.

Jason Johnson is now friends with Cassie Xxxxtasy.

Jason Johnson has not had time to vacuum, mow the lawn, or do the dishes. However, I did find time to pleasure myself to Cassie Xxxxtasy for the third time this afternoon.

Jason Johnson is now friends with Patrick Fuller.

Jason Johnson commented on Patrick Fuller's status.

Jason Johnson wants to ask Patrick Fuller: Seriously? You unfriended me, but kept that gay-bashing Ronald as your friend? I don't care if the guy is your son; he's a dick, plain and simple. And if you hadn't blocked me from your page, I'd let you know that.

Jason Johnson is now friends with Neal Renatta.

Jason Johnson is wondering why Neal Renatta wanted to be friends with me. I mean, I spoke to the guy maybe twice in high school, and as I recall, he was a total jackass. But I'm sure we'll have plenty to talk about.

Jason Johnson commented on Neal Renatta's photo.

Neal replied to **Jason Johnson**'s comment.

Jason Johnson isn't going to miss Neal Renatta's friendship. Guy's still a jackass.

Jason Johnson joined the group, *How fucking stupid IS Glen Beck anyway?!*

Jason Johnson now has 6 Facebook friends. Two are openly hostile, three are people whom I've never met but for some reason think I should buy their indie CD, and one is a sock puppet that I added myself so my friends list wouldn't look so damn pathetic.

Jason Johnson joined the group, *Thanks for Betty White, SNL, but it doesn't make up for all those shitty Molly Shannon sketches you made us sit through in the late 1990s.*

Jason Johnson is now friends with Bob Guntherson.

Jason Johnson likes Bob Guntherson's status.

Jason Johnson wants to make it clear that when I clicked the "like" button on Bob's status, it did NOT mean that I liked the fact that Bob had advanced testicular cancer.

Jason Johnson cannot imagine why any of his remaining friends think I could give a shit about what they had for breakfast, or their exercise regimen, or their stupid cat pictures. TOO MUCH INFO, folks!

Jason Johnson just had a bowel movement so big it was painful. I've uploaded a photo but one of you pricks complained to Facebook and they said it was a violation of their terms. I only have three friends left, and two of them want me to buy their indie CDs, so I'm looking at YOU, Dad!

Jason Johnson doesn't care that his own father unfriended him. You really think I don't know where you live, you senile old geezer?!

Jason Johnson commented on Jennifer Love Hewitt's photo.

SEE 178 SIMILAR POSTS

Jason Johnson thinks that booting him from Jennifer Love Hewitt's fan page is one thing, but why did I get a call from Homeland Security? NOT COOL.

Jason Johnson has joined the group, *You indie bands make me want to fucking puke.*

Jason Johnson thinks you so-called "friends" who are in indie groups are too damn sensitive to make it in the music business, or whatever you call that crap you play.

Jason Johnson spent yet another day at the lawyer's office, battling my ex-wife. I must've given that bitch about $9K before I realized that we had never been married.

Jason Johnson wants to know what happened to Cassie Xxxxtasy, and why her profile was suddenly replaced by a fat, hairy neocon dude that I don't remember ever friending.

Jason Johnson wants you to buy his new indie CD. And then look at some ugly pictures of my butt-faced baby. Now I'm sitting around watching *Hell's Kitchen*, which I think is SO fascinating that I need to share it with the world. See how YOU guys like it, you boring pieces of crap!

Jason Johnson hates you, and I'm not buying your CD or helping you pull crops for your damn Farmville game.

Jason Johnson has left Facebook.

WARNING: ARTICLE MAY CONTAIN BOOBS! BIG, FAT, BOOBS!

RECENTLY ABC AND FOX REFUSED to air a Lane Bryant lingerie commercial on the grounds that it showed "too much cleavage." Coincidentally, this is the same reason that CBS fired Dan Rather.

However, viewers suspected the real reason for the censorship is that the ad featured "plus-sized" model Ashley Graham, and the networks wanted to spare us the sight of a fat chick in her underwear. Needless to say, it set off a firestorm not seen since someone lit a match under Oprah's ass.

The networks were flooded with complaints that they were trying to suppress exposure of "real" women with "real" bodies. I'm not sure when the word "real" came to mean "fat," but it does explain at least three of the cast members of *Real Housewives of New Jersey*. They're certainly not "real" in any other sense.

I've watched the ad on YouTube, and I admit I'm torn on the issue. On one hand, it's a fairly tame ad by the standards of prime-time television. Or late afternoon television. Or by children's cartoon shows, especially if you include shows that were apparently designed to terrify children, like Regis Philbin.

Besides, as "plus-sized" models go, Ashley Graham is fairly decent-looking, and I could think of worse ways to go than to be smothered by that much boob. Seriously, I haven't seen jugs like that outside a hillbilly musical troupe. Even the Inquisition didn't use a rack that large.

On the other hand, I resent society's attempts to make obesity appear mainstream. Especially when we're facing an obesity epidemic in this country, and we look like whale carcasses bloating in the sun, unable to breathe from the weight of our bodies, until the Coast Guard decides to clear us out of the street with dynamite, sending pieces of our bloody blubber raining down on passers-by and parked cars like some grotesque, over-extended metaphor.

I also resent the phrase "plus-sized." I have no patience for euphemisms of any kind, unless by "plus" they mean, "lingerie model PLUS seventy pounds of lard."

It seems that, rather than face the fact that our asses now have the circumference of a NASCAR racetrack, we're supposed to believe that fat people are now attractive, something clearly disproven every day by Notorious BIG.

Jessica Simpson, Jennifer Love Hewitt, and Mariah Carey all had recent weight fluxes, and the PC crowd rushed to their defense, claiming they all still "looked great." But guess what? They all went on exercise programs. Why? *Because they knew they were fat*, like everyone else who owns a box of Twinkies and a mirror.

So they all lost the extra weight, and guess what? Everyone, including the PC crowd, thinks they're beautiful again. What's the story? Is Jessica Simpson hotter now, or was she hotter when she wore "Mom jeans" so big you could stuff a heifer into each leg?

Strangely, this is one area where men fare worse than

women. No one came to Al Gore's defense when he gained weight–he was just *fat*. And the Michelin Man hasn't gotten laid since the Ford administration.

So there are plenty of reasons why I should object to the Lane Bryant ad. But I have to reluctantly side with them on this weighty issue. Because Davy Jones' locker doesn't have a chest that big. I've seen smaller speed bumps in a Wal-Mart parking lot. Or, as Kemps ice cream would put it, it's the cows.

Hell, if I were a Sesame Street character, my muppet name would be Boobie Monster. I'd be a lot like Cookie Monster, except I'd see some massive fun bags and shout, "BOOOB-IES!" Then I'd go "nom nom nom nom nom," while stuffing them into my gullet (much of it would not go down my throat but would instead crumble off the sides of my mouth), brush off my lips, wave to Bert, and bob away, bemoaning the fact that I have no lower extremities.

Granted, this would preclude any more guest appearances by Katy Perry, but I think we can agree that that might be a good thing.

I'm done.

I WAS MOLESTED BY AL GORE

[*"It's-Not-Funny-If-I-Have-to-Explain-It" Dept: Al Gore was accused by a female masseuse of forcing her to drink cognac before coming after her like a "sex poodle." I'll leave it to astute readers to pick up on the other allegations made in her affidavit. I just didn't want people to think that I was inventive enough to make up this shit.*]

IT BEGAN WITH THE ERUPTION of that Icelandic volcano, which I think is called Kjlljyjluljyljk, or some other volcano that got its name in the traditional Icelandic way; i.e., a typist falling asleep on his keyboard after drinking too much tindavodka.

I was flying from New York to Oslo to attend a global warming conference and to have my pet lamb castrated for some mouth-watering sursadhir hrutspungar, a phrase that is actually easier to pronounce when your watery mouth is stuffed with lamb testicles.

Anyway, Europe was buried under an ash cloud worse than the one covering Drew Carey's living room, and my flight was canceled–not because of the ash cloud, but because it was an American Airlines flight, half of which have to be canceled as part of their quota.

So I decided to take a cab. Don't ask me how the drivers get from New York to Oslo. It probably involves the same method they use to make a 20-minute drive take two and a half hours.

I flagged down a cab, and because I'm not black, one of them stopped. But I found myself reaching the cab door at the same time as none other than Albert A. "None Other Than" Gore, whom I recognized from his successful film, which was, of course, *Transformers 2*. I believe he played the part of Megatron with minimal make-up.

We reached for the door at the same time. Our hands touched. Our eyes locked. And my head swooned, partly because I was in the presence of greatness, and partly because he had just pelted me in the face with his Nobel Prize.

But we eventually agreed to share the cab, and I spent the next few minutes adjusting to the mixed aromas of hummus and Grecian hair formula. I would then spend the next few hours adjusting to the aroma of greenhouse gasses coming from the former Veep.

Finally, I glanced over at Gore and noticed him giving me a "come-hither" look. Granted, I have in the past confused this look with his "go-thither" look, which I've also confused with his staring into space for hours at a time.

Then Gore reached into his briefcase, pulled out a bottle of cognac, and forced me to drink it. Of course, sometimes there's a fine line between "forcing" and "sharing," but you get the idea.

Pretty soon, Gore was all over me, groping me and French-kissing me like some kind of animal, like maybe… geez, I don't know…a hound dog? A pit bull? No, I got it: a crazed sex poodle. Yeah, that's it.

What are you looking at me like that for? I'm sticking with "sex poodle." Moving on.

He then tried to show me a pole that doesn't melt in the sunlight. "Mr. Gore, I'm not that type of girl," I told him, which should be obvious, despite my shapely breasts, broad hips, and monthly crotch bleeding.

But he continued the groping, kissing, and almost completely unsolicited sex. The rest of the details are too sordid for this paper, suffice it to say that it involves nudity, vulgarity, and the occasional pie chart.

After he left the cab, I checked my clothes and found them stained with his fluids. I decided not to launder them so I could prove my story. I later had them tested, and it was exactly what I thought it was: Grecian hair formula.

Why did I wait so long to come forward with this story? Because some Democratic "friends" of mine told me that bringing down Gore would help doom the planet. This explanation worked, because Gore is apparently Superman, and I'm kind of an idiot.

So I held off for the sake of the planet. But now that *Ugly Betty* has been canceled, I say the planet can go fuck itself.

Some accuse me of fabricating the story in order to capitalize on a brief meeting I had with the ex-Veep. That's a damn lie! I'm not doing this for money and notoriety– although, for another $1.5 million like *The Enquirer* is giving me, I'd sell out my own grandmother.

By the way, my grandma? Total sex poodle.

I'm done.

THE PENIS OR THE TRAIN: COMEDY TECHNIQUES REVEALED

ADIE NORFLEET, A VISUALLY IMPAIRED Atlantan woman, was recently reunited with the man who risked his life to save her after she walked off a train platform and into the path of an oncoming train, in what had to be the makings of the worst *Thomas the Tank Engine* episode ever.

Fortunately, a good samaritan jumped on the tracks and pulled Norfleet to safety. It was an act of heroism and bravery that I know that I, for one, could never have pulled off–mainly because I would've been too busy *laughing my ass off.*

I mean, c'mon: Not only does she walk straight off the platform, but the train is *on time*? What gods of Fate did she piss off, anyway? Did she recently say, "I wish to catch the train today" while holding a monkey paw?

I see your eyes glancing towards the comics page, so let me explain: A monkey paw grants you your wishes, but in a perverted, awful way; i.e., you wish to marry a wealthy celebrity, and soon you find yourself engaged to Mel Gibson.

Obviously, I'm being a little flippant about the woman's predicament. I'm sure that, once someone explained that the poor woman was visually impaired, I would've leapt into action:

"Here, ma'am, I'm going to throw you down something that you can grab onto and pull yourself up. Ready? OK, pull!...What's that? Yes, it *is* my penis. What, you're sitting in front of 70 tons of moving steel, and suddenly you're picky about the help? Penis or the train, lady!"

(Coincidentally, *Penis or the Train* was one of my favorite children's books.)

Now, lest anyone accuse me of advocating the sexual molestation of the handicapped, let me put you straight: I am absolutely opposed to it! Unless it's funny or convenient.

Ha ha ha! See? Again, that's another joke. That's how it works: I say funny stuff, and you laugh, unless you're that humorless blind woman whom I tricked into giving me a hand job.

No, no! There you go again! I didn't really trick a blind woman into– You know what? Perhaps I've not been doing a good enough job explaining satire. Let me talk about some of my recent work and show that, despite your reaction of nausea and high-pitched screaming, were really quite funny.

Take, for example, a recent column of mine in which I proposed the idea of making the Irish eat their own children. If one were to read the article closely, they would know that the idea is totally impractical, and hence humorous. To wit:

The Irish wouldn't eat children unless the children were potatoes. This is why so many Irish died during the potato famine of the 1840s as they stubbornly refused to boil up an infant.

In the column, I suggested grinding up children as young as eight years old. Again, clearly ridiculous. A child that size would never fit in the average kitchen grinder.

I further suggested that feed the children bovine growth hormones. We all know those hormones are too expensive to waste on drunken, dirty Irishmen.

See? None of what I said in that column should be taken seriously–except the part about Irish being a bunch of drunks. Really, do they think excessive drinking is going to make them feel better about sounding like a bunch of fruity Scottish-wannabes? I don't bloody think so.

And now I have to address you uptight bitches on my column about wife-beating. Again, extremely hilarious, if one considers:

I described the wife's head as making a "boing" sound when struck. The human head actually makes a wet "thud" sound–and besides, "boing" sounds are *always* funny.

I encouraged husbands to give their wives "a boot to the ass" if they don't put out. Again, any violence directed at the butt is inherently funny.

I encouraged husbands to grind up their wives and feed them to the Irish. Obviously, this could not be done, because who would be left to cook the children?

Finally, we come to my last column, in which I advocated solving the Social Security funding crisis by smothering the elderly with pillows. Now, that's hilarious because—

Come to think of it, that last one was out of line. I apologize unreservedly.

In fact, let me shake your hand and apologize. Yep, my hand is right out in front of you. Just grab it and shake.

I'm done.

LET'S HAVE A SERIOUS TALK ABOUT ALIEN RAPE

SAW AN AD FROM A young college-aged woman, who was making a student film about the paranormal. She requested stories about UFOs, psychic abilities, ghosts, and the walking dead, which presumably include Elvis and congressional Democrats.

Then she added the punch line: "Serious inquiries only."

One may rightly wonder how "serious" stories about UFOs are supposed to sound, when the typical submission reads, "I'm quite serious that E.T. anally raped me." I'd hate to be one of her neighbors when all those bullshit detectors go off.

According to one poll, about a third of the country believes in ghosts. Stranger still, most of them believe the ghosts were born in Kenya.

About a third believe in the existence of alien life on Earth, a surprisingly low figure, given the popularity of Snooki.

UFO invasions are largely accepted by those who have found themselves dumped into a mobile home collective sanctuary–i.e., trailer trash, upon whom the aliens have their way, leading scientists to believe that alien pheromones smell a lot like Budweiser and nachos.

One such backwater, uneducated hillbilly was Jimmy Carter, who once saw a UFO, and as president, urged NASA to look into the potential presence of alien life on Earth. It fell to NASA to explain to Carter that it was merely Governor Reagan.

And while you may laugh at these people for their beliefs—and I urge that you do so, repeatedly—it should be noted that 48% of people who believe in ESP are middle-class whites, who choose to remain middle class, rather than, say, having bought Microsoft stock in the early '80s.

"It doesn't work that way," they say. How did I know they were going to say that? Gee, maybe I'm psychic. Or maybe it's because that's what these ESP hucksters always say when confronted with their two divorces and home foreclosure.

Take Sylvia Browne, a self-proclaimed psychic who makes her living off the money of the gullible, which, to be fair, makes her little different from John Boehner.

She claims that she first realized that she was psychic when she dreamed that her great-grandmothers would die... and they *did*! Yes, only a psychic could predict the mortality of great-grandmothers. And by "psychic," I of course mean "anyone familiar with the stench of oncoming death."

Coincidentally, I was listening to a discussion on psychic phenomena on the radio last week. I won't say why I was listening, but it involves someone's clumsy hooker leaving the radio on during a particularly torturous bondage session.

In any case, the program interviewed a woman whose father she believed had precognition. So after she died, she did the only rational thing: She ate his brain.

Ha ha ha! No, of course not. That would be sick. She merely kept his skull.

No, really, she kept the skull. I bet her dad didn't see *that* coming. Because I think there would have been a bit more birth control in his misspent youth.

The show also had a segment on the phenomenon of crystal skulls, which are believed–often by people who have jobs in the crystal skull-selling business–to reduce stress, lower blood pressure, and reduce a fabulous Indiana Jones franchise into total crap.

The original crystal skulls were promoted by a 1920s carnie who claimed they were made by ancient Aztecs–or Mayans, if they're not the same thing. It was later claimed that only aliens could truly have sculptured them, even after vigorous denials of this by Gov. Reagan.

Speaking of wizened old skulls, Yoko Ono recently claimed that John Lennon's spirit is still with her. No word yet on whether his spirit is constantly shouting, "Stop selling my songs to shoe commercials, you stupid harpy!"

Another mummified pop star, Madonna, believes in the curative power of urine. This makes one wonder how anyone dies of kidney failure, or why the healthiest people in the world aren't unconscious drunks who spill that magic healing fluid all over their bodies. At the very least, their pants should magically mend themselves.

To be fair to all these kooks, I did have one psychic moment in my own life, and it even happened during the psychic-peddling show *Crossing Over*. As soon as it came on, I thought, "Well, *this* is going to be shit."

Psychic!

I'm done.

FAKE REEFER MADNESS!

HE CITY OF DULUTH HAS recently passed a ban on synthetic marijuana, which is synthetically designed to give one an imitation high after pretending to breathe it into one's artificial lung, resulting in the illusion that tax breaks for the wealthy benefit the poor.

So the Duluth "no fun anymore" city council has even begun taking away our pretend fun things. All I can say is, they'll have to pry my inflatable girlfriend from my cold, hairy-palmed hands.

Of course, it's unclear why anyone would want fake drugs, when the real things are so cheap and easy to obtain. Possibly it's because the imitation drugs give you an additional high from paying sales tax and helping to, say, pay the salaries of killjoy city council members.

Opponents have argued that the faux-marijuana results in violent behavior, which is not typically the result one sees from stoners, who generally spend their time contemplating the meaning of life before finding it at the bottom of the Chex Mix box.

By contrast, the imitation marijuana has provoked increased aggression, which has resulted in mood swings, violent assaults, and running as the Tea Party candidate for governor of New York.[1]

There are several brands of synthetic marijuana on the market, each with their own effect. Here are the names of some actual synthetic drugs on the market:

Voodoo Spice: Not to be confused with the least popular member of a 1990s British bubblegum group, this drug enables the user to raise your uncle from the dead to use as a drug mule. Has the downside of making people want to stick you with pins.

Blueberry Haze: Has the effect of making one blow up into a blueberry before being rolled off into a juicing room by Oompah Loompahs. Also makes people want to stick you with pins.

Hawaiian Hybrid: Makes user suddenly appreciate Don Ho. Potentially causes one to have a luau in the nude. There is no downside whatsoever.

Ninja: Gives one the feeling of being able to smash through a brick wall with one's head. Results include massive head trauma and a broken face. Again, no downside.

Magma: Thus named because it results in numerous embarrassing eruptions, if you catch my drift.

Skunk: Gives one the feeling of invincibility, and makes even the mightiest grizzly run away from you. Unfortunately, as you will learn too late, the same can not be said for highway traffic.

Genie: Gives one a hard-on for Barbara Eden. Can result in the rubbing of lamps, among other things.

Then there are the lesser-known synthetic drugs, possibly because I invented them while in a blueberry haze:

Junk in the Trunk: Will give user uncontrollable urge

---

1   Carl Palodino told a reporter, "I'll take you out." He ran on an "I'm angry" platform. Seriously.

to "shake it" and/or "back that thang up." Can result in being stalked by Sir Mix-a-Lot.

Eurocentric Blur: User will experience high colonialization impulses, followed by an inexplicable understanding of the metric system. Can make one forget that Africa exists.

Sweet Paradise: A drug that produces an intense state of euphoria, a feeling of flight, increased sexual stamina, and improved Sudoko scores. Followed up by six days of unstoppable rectal bleeding.

York Peppermint Patty: Gives one the feeling of being on a high mountaintop. Results in hypothermia and/or devouring by polar bears.

Golden Beck: Gives one the feeling of being a white MLK, and the sudden realization that "Glenn Beck" in the Hebrew alphabet spells out "Big Putz." It's true! Wake up, America! Can result in gold hoarding and lost sponsors.

Religion: Makes one believe that there is a Supreme Being guiding your destiny. You will give it all your money and pledge your soul to it. The crash comes hard and fast when you discover that the Being in question is character actor Wallace Shawn.

Some may accuse me of taking a sympathetic stand towards drugs because my audience is largely college-aged potheads who use reefers to ease the pain of no longer being able to park their third-generation Chevies on nearby residents' lawns.

And I know what they're saying: "You're selling out." And you know what I say: Old news. Because that's what it is. It's old news.

I'm done.

ABOUT THE DAMN AUTHOR

Jason Johnson is a contributor to the Duluth, MN-based *Zenith City Weekly*, for which he writes a column that no one reads. This is his third volume of essays, the previous two also having been unread and tossed into a dumpster behind a Goodwill store somewhere. He is a member of the Peanut Gallery Comics and the Peanut Gallery Musicians, whose unread and unheard gallery of crap can be found at facebook.com/peanutgallerycomics or myspace.com/peanutgallerycomics, or even myspace.com/peanutgallerymusicians. You pays your money; you gets your choice.